HELEN TSANOS SHEINMAN

# Love Laughter and lunch

The evocative memories of a Cypriot family's
journey recalled through traditional
Greek Cypriot recipes that are perfect for today

Food photographs: Antoine Bootz
Food stylist: Rebecca Omweg
Serifos photographs: Costas Picadas
Catalog photographs: Christopher Lawrence

Editorial director: Suzanne Slesin
Design: Stafford Cliff
Production: Dominick J. Santise, Jr.
Managing editor: Regan Toews
Assistant editor: Deanna Kawitzky

POINTED LEAF PRESS, LLC.
WWW.POINTEDLEAFPRESS.COM

# CONTENTS

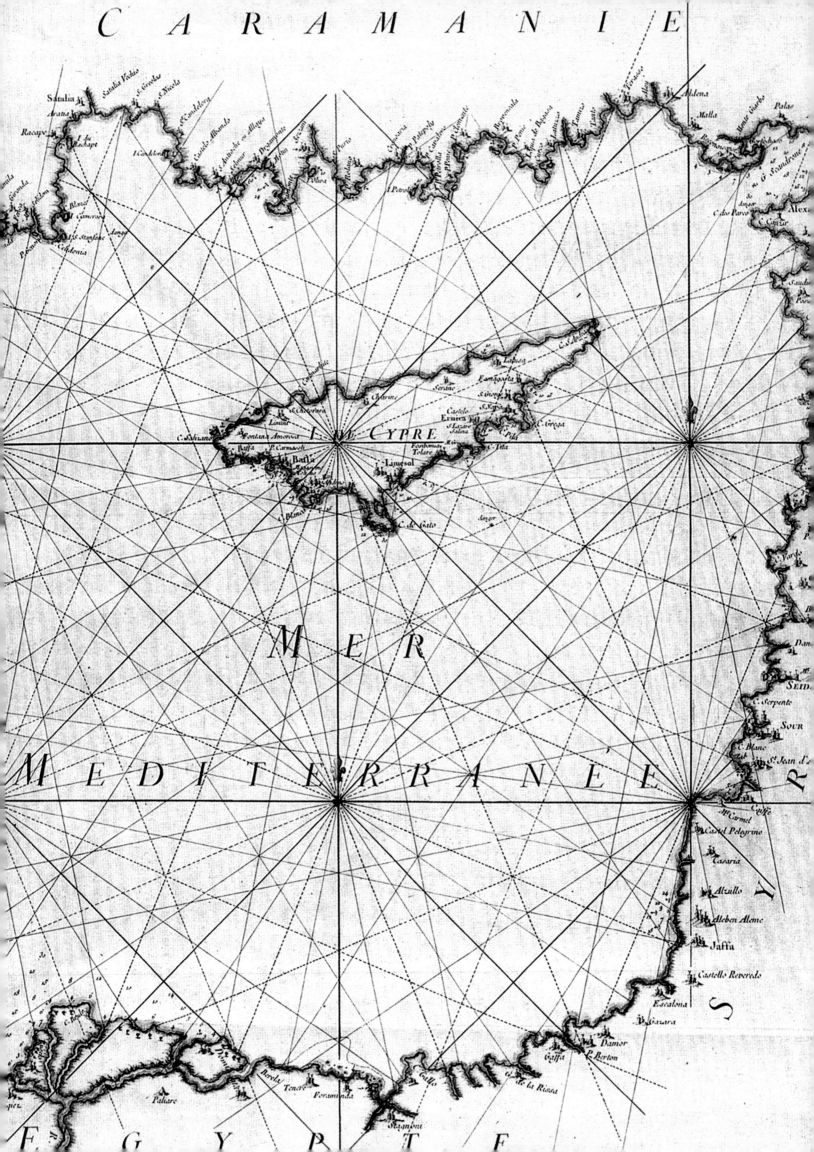

# 1: BEGINNING IN CYPRUS

Cyprus is the third largest island in the Mediterranean. This country, which has had its share of wars and political turmoil, is now divided between the Turkish north and the Greek south. The members of my family, who are of Greek heritage and lived in the north, had to abandon their homes at the time of the Turkish invasion in 1974, relocating to the south to start their lives over. For me, however, as a young girl who spent summer holidays there, Cyprus was a place of sunshine, blue skies, beaches, and food. I would stay for weeks at a time in the northern seaside resort of Famagusta, where my father's side of the family lived, including my paternal grandparents, Lysandros and Despina, and my aunts, Eveltha and Maroulla. I loved listening to their stories, and I learned unusual things, such as how to predict the future from coffee grounds. Whenever we wanted to visit my mother's side of the family, we would drive to Agios Dometios in Nicosia, the capital, to find Papou Kouli. He was always in the kafenio, or coffee shop, playing cards or backgammon. In Cyprus, I ate grapes plucked straight from the vine and picked fresh figs and oranges from the garden. Food was always a main focus—whether kleftiko, makaronia tou fournou, or louvi. They were always absolutely delicious. All the women in my family were comfortable in their spotless kitchens, constantly preparing meals. They decorated their dining and living rooms with beautiful textiles that we, as children, were warned never to touch. Having now learned the special skills and techniques required to create these exquisite pieces of fabric, I understand why they protected them so carefully. In August, when the weather became too hot, we would drive up to the Troodos Mountains. I'll never forget the smell of herbs growing wild along the sides of the roads. Sometimes we would stop and pick chamomile to make tea, or lavender to put under our pillows for restful nights. I was sad never to have met my maternal grandmother, Eleni, as she died during childbirth. Having become close with all her children, my uncles and aunts, I am certain that she was a beautiful, hard-working, and skilled woman to have survived as long as she did, with eight children to feed and care for. Spending time every summer with my family all those years ago in Cyprus taught me many things. It gave me insight into how love and the simple things in life are the most nurturing of all. As an adult, even in the most trying of times, I am able to connect with a time when sunny days were endless and love was unconditional.

OPPOSITE Cyprus is shown in an antique map before its 1974 partition into the Republic of Cyprus, which today comprises 59% of the island's area, excluding the Turkish-controlled north.

Uncle Lefteris

Aunty Hrisi

Aunty Maroulla

Aunty Eveltha

Yia Yia

Papou

Adam

Lysandros

PREVIOUS PAGES My mother and I—neither of us good swimmers—stayed in the shallow water the first summer I spent in Famagusta, when I was about six years old.

As a child, I was told countless stories about my paternal grandparents, each more exciting to me than the last. I would eagerly await the chance to sit around the table with the adults and listen as they shared memories over Othello red wine, Marlboro Light cigarettes and a card game called gounga, or Cypriot rummy. From these stories, each told on various occasions and recounted by different members of the family, it became clear to me that my paternal grandfather, Lysandros, was a very emotional and headstrong man. They say he married the Varossi town beauty—who as a young girl had that stark combination of deep blue eyes and jet black hair—not because he wanted a wife, but out of jealousy at the prospect of another man marrying her first. He was so possessive of my grandmother that he would never let her out of his sight. His domineering nature extended far beyond his wife, and was also visible in the way he treated his daughters. Despite the fact that they lived on the beach, my aunts were never allowed to wear bathing suits, as their father feared such attire would reveal too much of their figures. As a result, the two of them never learned to swim, and even today they don't dare go in the water! In the few years I was able to spend with my grandfather during his life, I, too, fell subject to his somewhat endearing overprotectiveness. I have a distinct memory of a visit I paid him in Famagusta when I was 15 or 16 years old. Whenever we were out for a stroll, my grandfather would always insist that I walk three to four feet in front of him, giving him a vantage point from which to watch over me and keep away any boy who would so much as look at me. As for my grandmother, Yia Yia Despina, the first thing I think of is the long, thick braid that she wore bound up around her head. She would regularly take down the firm knot before going to bed, revealing a flowing, feminine mane of black hair. I remember being shocked at how much younger and freer she looked whenever I managed to catch sight of her at night. Although she lost much of her eyesight early on in life, she nevertheless managed to keep her house immaculately shiny. When I was in Cyprus during the summers, my favorite time of day to visit her house was in the early afternoon. For it was at this time that, as she swept and hosed down her verandas for the second time of the day, she would tell me all of her childhood stories.

OPPOSITE My father's father, Lysandros, grandfather or Papou to me, and my father's mother, Despina or Yia Yia to me, each hold one of their grandchildren: my first cousins, Adam and Lysandros. Behind them stand my uncle Lefteris and his wife Hrisi, and on either side of them are two of my aunts, Eveltha and Maroulla. My father Yiannakis was the second of six children—Lakis, Lefteris, and Loizos were his brothers, and Maroulla and Eveltha, his two sisters.

ABOVE The photograph of my mother, Agnes, as a baby, sitting on her father's lap, is the earliest one I have of her. The little boy is her brother, my uncle Stelios, who retired to Cyprus after spending many years in London. My grandfather, Papou Kouli, lived in Cyprus his entire life. As children, my brothers and I would tease him about his big ears.

My grandmother, Despina, would always tell me which herbs would best cure any headache, stomach pain, or cold that I had. The more Greek literature and mythology I read, the more I have grown to understand that her herbal remedies were actually rooted in the texts of ancient Greek scientists and philosophers, *overleaf*.

## ROSEMARY:

In the ancient world, rosemary was considered an aid to memory. It was also believed to bring success to any undertaking and thus small sprigs were always inserted into a bride's bouquet to ensure a happy marriage. Rosemary is used in abundance when cooking lamb and fish.

## BASIL:

Greek folklore tradition connects basil with Agia Eleni, a saint who is especially dear to me, as she is my namesake in Greek. It is said that when Eleni went to ancient Palestine looking for Christ's cross, she came across a sweet-smelling shrub and thought it was a sign of God. She dug under its root and found the cross. This herb has many uses but is especially delicious with tomato dishes and, of course, in pesto sauce.

## MINT:

According to Greek mythology, Minthe was a beautiful Nymph whom the god Pluto had fallen in love with, and so he changed into this aromatic plant to escape the jealously of his wife. Mint's health benefits include treating gallstones and the common cold. It is popular in hot or cold tea and can be added to fruit salads. It is also an ingredient in body lotions and oils.

## CORIANDER, CILANTRO or KOLIANDROS:

This herb was made into an ointment with other herbs to soothe pain in the joints. It is one of the most popular ingredients in Cypriot cuisine. Both the fresh leaves and dried seeds are used extensively in salads, pastas, meat, and fish.

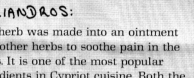

## THYME:

In ancient Greece, thyme— because of its pungent fragrance—was used as both an incense to purify the air and as an antiseptic to cure colds, coughs, even whooping cough. Today, it is used to flavor soups, stews, and lamb.

## SAGE:

In antiquity, sage had the reputation of being the most important herb of all, as it was believed to be able to ward off death. Sage leaves were used to help the immune system and to boost memory by strengthening the brain. Due to its strong scent, it should be used in moderation in cooking, but is delicious when added to pasta and fish.

## OREGANO or RIGANI:

Traditionally, Hippocrates, the father of medicine, recommended this herb in cases of afflictions of the eyes, toothaches, and digestive and respiratory problems. These days, it is mostly used in the form of dry leaves to season baked or grilled fish, along with olive oil and lemon. My teenage cousins from London love this herb sprinkled over french fries!

I recently had the good fortune to be invited to participate in a television program about traditional and modern Cypriot art and industry. It was very exciting to go back to Cyprus with the purpose of researching this topic, during the course of which I was thrilled to be given the opportunity to meet some contemporary artisans. Textiles and handicrafts are a huge part of Cypriot culture, and are really demonstrative of the creativity and refined techniques that continue to thrive. It made me especially happy to see that Cypriot women, young and old alike, continue to build on these ancient techniques and traditional designs with such pride in their heritage. Cyprus has a long tradition of women weaving and embroidering. The fabrics were usually crafted by mothers for their daughters' trousseaux, but could also provide an additional source of income. It was customary for mothers to teach their daughters how to prepare the raw materials, weave them on the loom, and sew the fine embroidery.

OPPOSITE Cypriot woven and embroidered textiles come in a variety of designs, as each village is identified by its unique color combinations and motifs. The fabrics from Phyti, a village on the west coast of the Paphos area, are called Phythkiotika. These are very easy to identify, as they are embroidered with bright oranges, yellows, reds, and blues, and are decorated with geometric designs such as diamonds, squares, and triangles. I love to visit Phyti when I am in Cyprus, as there is a wonderful folk art and textile museum in the village.

RIGHT The traditional and vividly colored clothing worn by both men and women was often embellished with intricate designs and worn for special occasions, such as weddings and feast days. On work days, the clothing would be less ornamented, even though one could still see a woman wearing a beautifully embroidered head scarf.

OPPOSITE I was very excited to find these colorful placemats in the village of Phyti. The mats and the hand-painted plates remind me so much of spring in Cyprus—the green of the hills and the oranges and magentas of the wild flowers are everywhere at that time of year. The preparation of food—a focal point of Cypriot culture—sitting around a family table, and setting the table have become crucial parts of the Greek Cypriot meal. The manner in which a table is set and the way in which each dish is presented is something I was taught to care about since I was a child. "It has to be pleasing to the eye so that the appetite grows bigger!" my parents would always say to me as they taught me how to set a beautiful table for one of our dinners. I simply can't think about Cyprus without thinking about halloumi! It is the first thing I want to eat when I arrive, and the last thing I want to taste before I leave. Halloumi is a traditional cheese made from goat- and sheep's-milk. The milder versions resemble mozzarella in taste and consistency, but the aged kind is my personal favorite, as it is much stronger and saltier. The great thing about halloumi is that it can be prepared in so many ways and combined with such varied ingredients, making it a really versatile food for any kind of meal. I especially like to eat it freshly cut, along with a delicious piece of sweet watermelon. This combination is often served for breakfast during the hot summer months in Cyprus.

RIGHT Halloumi cheese may be grilled and served warm—always put lots of lemon on it while it is still hot—or grated and used on pasta instead of parmesan, or cubed and tossed cooked or uncooked into a salad. One of my favorite dishes consists of halloumi with thinly sliced fennel, fresh coriander, mint leaves, and arugula, topped with good olive oil and plenty of lemon.

# KLEFTIKO · "STOLEN MEAT"

According to legend, this meat would be made with lamb stolen by bandits in the mountains who needed to cook without being caught. They would place the meat for many hours in a hole in the ground, sealed with mud, so that no steam could escape to give away their whereabouts.

SERVES 4

INGREDIENTS:

Juice of 2 lemons
Handful of roughly chopped fresh oregano and mint leaves
2 split cloves of garlic
Fresh ground pepper
Sea salt
4 8oz leg of lamb steaks or chops with bones
3 tbsps extra virgin olive oil
3 medium-sized onions thinly sliced
5-6 bay leaves
2-3 cups of dry white wine

METHOD:

Mix the lemon juice, oregano and mint leaves, garlic, fresh ground pepper and salt and pour over lamb (both sides). Cover and store at room temperature or in refrigerator. Leave to marinate for at least 2 hours if you can. Drain lamb, but retain marinade. Pat lamb dry with paper towel. Preheat oven to 325°F. Heat olive oil in large pan and brown lamb on both sides. (I like to add a little more salt at this point). Transfer the lamb into a shallow ovenproof dish. After removing the lamb, add the onions to the pan and cook until softened. They will pick up the brown "fond" from the bottom of the pan. Add this and the wine to the reserved marinade and lamb.

Combine in oven proof dish and cover. Roast for 2 hours turning meat every 30 minutes and adding water if juices start to evaporate.

The meat should be tender and served with the onions and all their juices.

# Louvana Soup
## (Yellow Split Pea Soup)

Serves 4-6.

This is the easiest and most deliciously exotic soup to make. It is a wonderful, vibrant yellow color and I have always received such rave reviews from my friends when I have served it at dinner parties.

2 cups yellow split peas
Water of chicken stock to cover peas by three inches
Salt/pepper
1 cup Long Grain Rice
4-6 Yellow onions, medium in size, finely chopped
3/4 cup lemon juice
1/2 cup good quality olive oil
5 sprigs of oregano or thyme (optional)

Wash the split peas and place in casserole. Cover with water. Add a little salt. Bring to boil and then change the water, filling up to about 3 inches above peas. Continue to cook on medium heat. Once water has come back up, simmer until peas feel "al dente," about 25-30 minutes.

Add the rice and cook for an additional 10-15 minutes or until both peas and rice are cooked to the same consistency, stirring occasionally. Switch off. You want the rice and peas to be floating in the liquid so it looks like a thickish soup.
Heat the olive oil in a pan and add the onions. Sauté until the onions are very brown (the browner the sweeter). Once sautéed, turn heat off and add the lemon juice. Add entire mixture to soup, including the oil, and serve.

Steep sprigs of oregano or thyme in the soup for about 10 minutes (optional)

I like to garnish this soup with a thin slice of lemon in the center of bowl.

# FAGGI (LENTILS WITH RICE)

SERVES 6 AS A SIDE DISH

2 CUPS   BROWN LENTILS, WASHED
1 CUP    LONG GRAIN RICE
6 ONIONS
$\frac{1}{2}$ CUP LEMON JUICE
2 BAY LEAVES
OLIVE OIL
SALT / PEPPER TO TASTE

SLICE ONIONS AND CARAMELIZE IN LARGE SAUTÉ PAN ON MEDIUM HEAT WITH A LITTLE OLIVE OIL AND SALT. COOK AS LONG AND SLOW AS YOU CAN, ADDING $\frac{1}{4}$ CUP OF WATER AT A TIME TO PREVENT BURNING. THE LONGER YOU COOK THEM, THE SWEETER THEY WILL BE. WHEN ONIONS ARE VERY TENDER AND A RICH GOLDEN BROWN, ADD LEMON JUICE AND SET ASIDE.

WHILE ONIONS ARE COOKING, RINSE LENTILS AND COVER WITH TWICE AS MUCH WATER IN A MEDIUM SAUCE PAN. BRING TO A BOIL, THEN STRAIN AND CHANGE WATER. ADD 2 BAY LEAVES AND SIMMER UNTIL JUST TENDER, ABOUT 20 MINUTES.

WHILE LENTILS ARE COOKING, SIMMER THE RICE ACCORDING TO PACKAGE DIRECTIONS. WHEN FINISHED, REMOVE FROM HEAT. LET SIT FOR 10 MINUTES, COVERED. FLUFF WITH FORK.

THEN IN A LARGE BOWL COMBINE WITH LENTILS AND ONIONS WITH ALL THE LEMON JUICE AND OIL. ADD SALT AND PEPPER, AND MIX.

# LOUVI (BLACK-EYED BEANS WITH GREEN CHARD)

CHARD LEAVES ARE BEST TO USE IN THIS RECIPE, BUT SPINACH OR ZUCCHINI SLICES, OR A COMBINATION OF ALL THREE, ALSO WORK REALLY WELL.

SERVES 4-6.

2 CUPS BLACK-EYED BEANS, SOAKED OVERNIGHT (YOU MUST ADD AT LEAST DOUBLE THE AMOUNT OF WATER TO BEANS AS THE BEANS SOAK UP ALL THE WATER)

1 lb.  CHARD LEAVES, WASHED THOROUGHLY, STEMS REMOVED
       OLIVE OIL
       JUICE OF 1 LEMON
       SALT /PEPPER TO TASTE

PLACE BEANS IN A SAUCEPAN AND COVER WITH FRESH WATER. BRING TO BOIL, DRAIN AND RINSE.

RETURN THE BEANS TO THE SAUCEPAN, COVER WITH MORE FRESH WATER AND BRING TO A GENTLE SIMMER, SO AS NOT TO HAVE THE BEANS FALL APART - ABOUT 25-30 MINUTES, OR UNTIL THE BEANS ARE ALMOST TENDER, ADDING A LITTLE EXTRA WATER IF NECESSARY TO KEEP THE BEANS COVERED.

SHRED THE GREENS AND STIR INTO BEANS AND COOK FOR A FURTHER 3-4 MINUTES. (IF USING CHARD, REMEMBER TO REMOVE STEMS.)

SEASON WITH SALT AND PEPPER. DRAIN AND SERVE IN SOUP BOWLS. DRIZZLE WITH OLIVE OIL AND LEMON JUICE.

THIS CAN BE SERVED ALONE WITH SOME DELICIOUS BREAD, OLIVES AND RAW ONIONS, OR SERVED AS A SIDE DISH TO A FISH ENTRÉE.

# Makaronia Tou Fournou
## (Also known as Pastitsio)

**For the ground meat:**

1½ lb  Lean minced beef
1 onion finely chopped
½ cup of dry white wine
½ cup of corn oil
1 tbsp of parsley finely chopped
1 cup of ripe tomatoes finely chopped
1 tsp of tomato paste
Salt/pepper

**For the Béchamel Sauce:**

5 cups of fresh whole milk
½ cup of flour
½ cup of butter
4 egg yolks
½ cup grated halloumi cheese
½ tsp of nutmeg
Salt/pepper

**For the Pasta:**

1½ lb thick macaroni
1 cup  grated halloumi cheese
          (can use kefalotiri)
½ tsp  mint
½ tsp  cinnamon
¼ tsp  nutmeg
2 tsp  olive oil
Salt/pepper

Prepare the ground-meat mixture first. Heat oil in a frying pan and add onions. When onions are soft, add the meat and stir until the meat is light brown. Pour in the wine and when it boils, add parsley, tomatoes, salt, pepper and tomato paste. Stir, cover and simmer on a low heat for about 30 minutes.

For the béchamel cream, warm milk in a saucepan. Melt butter in another pan and add flour to it slowly. Stir constantly with a whisk until mixture becomes a thick paste. Now take the heated milk and little by little add to the flour, stirring constantly until it becomes a thick cream (this must be done carefully to avoid any lumps). Remove from heat and add the egg yolks, grated cheese, nutmeg, salt & pepper.

To prepare the macaroni, boil water in a pot, adding salt and olive oil and then the macaroni. Cook for about 6-8 minutes and stir a few times so pasta does not stick. Drain and put in large bowl. Add pepper, mint, cinnamon, nutmeg and 3 tbsps of the finished béchamel and mix well. Grease your baking dish with butter all around. Add a thick layer of the macaroni. Sprinkle some grated cheese and cover with half the cream. Add the meat and the rest of the macaroni on top. Cover with remaining béchamel and sprinkle with grated cheese.
Bake in preheated oven (350°F) for about 45 minutes or until top is golden brown and the rest is cooked through.

Remove from oven, let cool and carefully cut into squares.
Makaronia can be served hot or cold.

# MAHALEPI
## CUSTARD WITH ROSE WATER AND CARDAMOM
### SERVES 4-6

| | |
|---|---|
| 4 CUPS | WHOLE MILK |
| 3 TBSP | SUGAR |
| 3 TBSP | CORNSTARCH |
| 1 TBSP | GROUND CARDAMOM |
| 2-3 TSP | ROSE SYRUP |
| 2-3 TSP | ROSE WATER |
| ½ CUP | PISTACHIO NUTS |
| PINCH OF SALT | |

IN A SMALL BOWL, DISSOLVE CORNSTARCH WITH A FORK INTO A LITTLE MILK AND PUT REMAINING MILK IN A POT WITH THE SUGAR, SALT AND CARDAMOM. TURN ON HEAT AND WHEN MILK IS WARM (SHOULD SEE STEAM RISING OFF THE MILK), NOT BOILING, WHISK IN CORNSTARCH MIXTURE. SIMMER UNTIL THE MIXTURE BECOMES CREAMY, STIRRING CONSTANTLY.

ADD ROSE WATER AND TURN OFF HEAT. TURN INTO BOWLS AND ALLOW TO COOL.
REFRIGERATE UNTIL IT THICKENS TO A CUSTARD CONSISTENCY. SPRINKLE WITH TOASTED PISTACHIO NUTS AND DRIZZLE WITH THE ROSE WATER SYRUP FOR COLOR AND ADDED TASTE.

THIS CUSTARD CAN BE SERVED COLD OR CAN BE LEFT WARM AND NOT ALLOWED TO THICKEN, POURED OVER FRESH FIGS AND PEACHES.

The Kafenio, or café, has always played a big role in Cypriot life. Usually located in the main square of the town, the Kafenio is where locals would gather to drink coffee, play games like tavli or backgammon, or just sit and watch the world go by. The latest news and gossip of the village—births, deaths, and marriages were at the top of the list—were first heard at the Kafenio. While it was open to all, it was usually the domain of men, while the women would meet in each others' homes.

## HOW TO MAKE CYPRIOT COFFEE

When I was growing up, Greek coffee was known as Turkish coffee. But due to the conflict of 1974, when Turkey invaded Cyprus, it is now considered politically incorrect to call this coffee, which is exactly the same, anything but Greek. Making Greek coffee was considered a rite of passage in the kitchen. One was taught at a young age, and once the technique had been mastered, one was allowed to make it for the grown-ups. I remember being 13 years old when my father finally congratulated me on the perfect cup! Greek coffee is served in three ways: Sketo, or plain and without sugar; metrio, or medium with one teaspoon of sugar; and glyko, or sweet, with two spoons of sugar. The coffee is usually made in a special pot called the briki, and is served with foam on top while the grounds remain at the bottom. The briki comes in two-, four-, and six-demitasse cup sizes. Using a demitasse cup as a measure, pour the desired amount of water into the pot, adding the coffee and sugar, if desired—for every cup of water, use one heaping spoon of coffee. Put over a medium to low heat and stir constantly until the coffee has dissolved. Continue to heat slowly until the foam starts to rise. The richer the foam, called kaimaki, the better the coffee. This was the tricky part to learn as a young girl. When the foam rises to the top, remove the pot quickly from the heat and serve. Evenly divide the foam among the cups and then fill them with the remainder of the coffee. Greek coffee is served very hot, accompanied by a glass of cold water.

## READING COFFEE GROUNDS

When I was young and would visit my grandmother Despina, I loved waiting for everyone to finish their coffee so I could bring the cups to her to read their tichi, or good fortune, by looking at the coffee grounds. My grandmother was so good at fortune-telling that people from the neighborhood would come to have a coffee with her so that they could have their cups read by her afterwards.

# 2: Moving to London

Growing up in London was special. Growing up in a Cypriot household in London was even more special. My parents met there in 1955 and got married the following year. I still recognize many faces from their wedding photograph. While some of them have passed away, others are still here—looking older, of course. Yet each of them continues to influence the way in which I have brought up my two daughters, Alexia and Isabel. Aunty Nitsa was the perfect second mother, serving me toast in bed on Sunday morning; Aunty Xenia, always optimistic, taught me to have a skip in my step every single day; and Uncle Mikis gave me advice when, afraid of hurting my parents' feelings, I went to him with my problems. These memories come from the time we lived in Wood Green, North London, where a large Cypriot community had settled. My teenage years were spent in Hadley Wood, a beautiful part of Hertfordshire just on the northern outskirts of London. Though we lived in other houses in between, these are the two homes I feel most connected to. Our life in Hadley Wood was very happy. My parents were healthy and full of fun and laughter. We had music and parties every weekend, and each holiday was an excuse for a huge celebration. Our kitchen was always filled with food and people cooking. I still remember the aromas that went through the house. It was there that I learned the meaning of true hospitality. Growing up with 30 first cousins, we were always going to a wedding. No matter whom we married, our weddings celebrated our Cypriot heritage. The dishes dedicated to my father, John Pitharas Tsanos, my mother, Agnes Hadjigeorgiou Pitharas Tsanos, and my brothers, Lysandros and George Tsanos, are the ones I always make with them in mind. I loved and continue to love them all deeply.

OPPOSITE A contemporary map of London shows Green Lanes, a long street that runs through a neighborhood of Greeks and Cypriots.

ΧΕΙΡΑ ΔΕΙΓΜΑΤΑ

PREVIOUS PAGES My mother was never one to wear her heart on her sleeve in public, so her smile here speaks volumes about her joy at her wedding, which was held in London in 1955 at the Agios Pandous Greek Orthodox Church. I can imagine the happiness she must have felt, as my father represented a new and exciting beginning for her in every way. He was handsome and smart, and had a contagious energy about him. He was unlike anyone that my mother had known in her own family, where the constant struggle for survival took precedence over intellectual curiosity and familial love.

LEFT We moved into this house—or, as we called it, "Our White House"—in 1967, when I was 11 years old. I remember being so excited to be living in Hadley Wood, Hertfordshire, a beautiful suburb of North London. We were the first of our extended family to live in such an exclusive neighbor-hood and it made us feel very special. I particularly loved the lions that sat out front, because, along with my brothers, Lysandros, who was then nine years old, and five-year-old George, I used to pretend that they were watch guards that would protect us at night.

LEFT My mother and Lysan-dros, when he was about two-and-a-half years old, were sitting on the wall of our first house in Wood Green, North London. Lysandros always had a very special connection with my mother—the two under-stood each other without ever having to say a word.

OPPOSITE My first cousins, Koula and Gina—standing next to me with their backs against the wall, and who are still like sisters to me—and Lysandros, in front, are in the middle of a game my father most likely invented for us.

Although my parents were adamant about having dinners together as a family at home, they also believed that eating out with friends was important, as it exposed us to different cuisines and to the finer things in life. As a family, we would often travel to the center of London to go to the theater or a concert. A gourmet dinner at Wheeler's—the best fish restaurant at the time, where I learned to eat perfectly prepared Dover sole—would often follow. This was a far cry from the upbringing that my parents had been used to when they were children growing up in Cyprus. Education was something that both of my parents really valued, as neither of them had had the opportunity or the means to receive a university degree of any kind. My mother had left school at the age of 11, when her own mother died, and, as the oldest girl of the family, she had to go to work to help support her seven siblings. My brilliant father was completely self-taught. He loved words and delighted in the hours he spent reading the dictionary to study new ones. He would always tell us: "Education is the one thing you give yourself that nobody can ever steal, buy, or take away." I cherish the philosophical talks and debates that we always had around the dinner table, whether at home or in a fine restaurant. It is an example I have tried to set for my own family. The exchange of ideas and thoughtful dialogue, accompanied by a truly delicious meal, of course, is my idea of ultimate bliss.

ABOVE LEFT, LEFT, AND OPPOSITE The pictures of my parents eating out with their siblings, cousins, and friends remind me of how I used to sit in my mother's bedroom while she would get dressed and prepare for a night on the town. Both my parents had beautiful clothes during this time and enjoyed wearing them. The Elysée on Percy Street and Jimmy's on Frith Street were two of their favorite restaurants because of their excellent Cypriot food and live Greek music.

My father was my first and best teacher. His success lay in the fact that he taught us not by being a disciplinarian, but by becoming a student with us. Whenever he wanted us to learn something new, he would also join in on the lessons in Greek dancing, karate, music, language, and debating. My dad was, above all, a lover of the written word. His own interest and enthusiasm rubbed off on us—we loved to sit with him and learn the etymological roots and meanings of words. Every Sunday during lunch—which was never shorter than three-hours—my brothers and I each had to come prepared to debate a topic of our choice. My father made a lot of fun out of what could have been a tiresome task. We covered every subject imaginable—some serious, others very funny. Dad was also a great orator and was always the center of attention at a party, never failing to entertain a crowd with colorful anecdotes and jokes. He was a true talent, and always had a twinkle in his eye that made it impossible to discern whether he was being serious or not. A philosopher at heart, my father could never settle with just one answer to any question, and he made sure that we felt the same. We always had to look at things from all angles, taking into consideration the scientific, political, philosophical, and psychological aspects to each and every question. He had a low tolerance for people who were stuck with their own limited views, and he never stopped emphasizing how important it was to be curious in life. It was this same curiosity and enthusiasm that landed him in a number of highly unique careers. As a young man, his goal was to become a lawyer, so he spent his days performing various menial jobs to put himself through night school. It soon became very clear, however, that my father was far more apt at using his mind than he was with his hands. Although he was too stubborn and proud to ever admit it, he was an absolutely terrible craftsman. Once, when he was working for a pipe

manufacturer, he was asked by the owner to come in early the following day. He practically skipped home that afternoon, convinced that he was about to be given a promotion. He asked my mother to iron his good shirt and pair of trousers and insisted on celebrating by spending his past day's earnings on taking her out to a nice dinner. The next morning, he woke up earlier than usual, eager to get to the office to hear the good news. Desperately trying to hide his cheeky smile, he was to learn that he was, in fact, not being promoted but fired! Apparently, in the short week that he had worked there, instead of reproducing the prototype to which he had been assigned, his lack of eye and hand coordination contributed to a differently designed pipe every day—exactly what his employer did not want. It took a few more similar situations before he finally found a profession that suited him. He and my mother started a clothing manufacturing company. Mum was the seamstress, Dad was the salesman. Over time, the small company grew into one of the most successful fashion manufacturing companies in London. My father's charm (and, of course, my mother's incredible dexterity on the sewing machine) made them the favored manufacturer for clothing worn by Twiggy, one of the most iconic fashion models of the time. Now that I am a parent myself, I wish I had my father around to share my joy and to see the outcome of his lessons. He died suddenly of a heart attack when I was pregnant with my second daughter, Isabel, without having had the chance of getting to really know his grandchildren or seeing me blossom as a mother.

LEFT Our family often played board games in the living room of our house in Hadley Wood. I was 11 years old, Lysandros was eight, and George was four when this photograph was taken for a newspaper article. The coffee table is now in my living room in New York.

# Red Snapper in Parchment

My father loved fish and two of his favorite ingredients were capers and olives. I know this would be a recipe he would really have enjoyed had he still been alive today.

2 red snapper fillets, about 8oz each

1/4 cup of extra virgin olive oil

4 bay leaves

1 1/2 tsp whole pink peppercorns

2 tbsp capers, rinsed

2 tbsp pomegranate seeds

1/2 cup black olives, pitted & halved

Juice of 2 lemons

1/4 cup dry white wine

Lemon wedges

Salt | pepper

Parchment paper

Combine the lemon juice, oil, bay leaves, capers, peppercorns, wine and olives in a large bowl.
Add the red snapper to the marinade, cover and refrigerate for at least 2 hours.

Preheat oven. Take a shallow sauté pan. Remove snapper from marinade and pat very dry, reserving the marinade. Place snapper in pan, add a little more olive oil (enough to thinly coat pan) and sauté on high heat for 3-4 minutes. Remove. Brush parchment paper (which has been cut to size) with a little olive oil and place fillet in the middle.
Add the marinade, salt, pepper, lemon wedges and pomegranate on top. Close packet by tying with a string on top, leaving an air pocket.
Bake for 10-12 minutes. Serve the fish in paper.

Papou Lysandros

Aunty Ellou

Yiayia Despina

Elpiniki

Eleftheria

Aunty Evektha

STELIOS

AGNES MY MUM

AUNTY MAROULLA

AUNTY ANGELLOU

My mother has always had a weakness for olive bread. She would be happy to eat a meal of olives and bread every day of her life. It was because of her that we had an abundance of homemade breads and a selection of olives at every meal. Her other biggest joy in life was, and continues to be, music. She was blessed with a beautiful voice—our friends would say that she had the voice of a nightingale. As a child, I remember her singing all day and night. Although she considered herself lucky to have been given this gift of music and song, the truth is that music was really her gift to us. While Greek was my first language, I only came to adore it from listening to my mother sing the poetic love songs of Marinella and Sophia Vembo—two of the most popular Greek singers at that time—over and over while she worked in the kitchen. I think this is why, years later, I find myself always needing to have music playing in the background when I cook. For some people, certain smells spark memories of their youth, but for me, some songs immediately transport me back to my mother, her food, and my teenage years. Even while she cooked, she would speak, melodically, to her food. She often told my siblings and I: "If you talk to your food, it will talk back to you in taste and flavor." She instilled in me the same habit of devotion and passion for cooking any dish, insisting that the same attention be applied to every meal, whether it be a simple breakfast of eggs and grilled halloumi cheese, her more complicated spinach and leek pie, or even her beloved olive bread. It is true that over the years, when I have taken great care to prepare food for a dinner party, I have witnessed my guests become more and more impassioned in their conversations as the meal progressed from the first to the final course. It is as if, with each bite they took, they absorbed all of the love and delight that went into preparing the meal.

LEFT During one of her summer holidays in Famagusta, my mother Agnes, in the white dress, was photographed with my father's parents, Despina and Lysandros. The two girls kneeling at the center of the group are my father's sisters, aunty Eveltha and aunty Maroulla, who are surrounded by their cousins.

# Agnes' Olive Bread

Once upon a time, the only place we would ever think about eating olive bread was fresh out of my mother's oven. Living now in New York City, whenever I see olive bread in a grocery store, it always puts a smile on my face, as it reminds me of my mother, happily singing in the kitchen, her hands lovingly kneading away to create her delicious homemade olive bread.

## For the Dough:

5 cups plain flour

2 teaspoons baking powder

1 cup olive oil

$1\frac{1}{3}$ - $1\frac{1}{2}$ cups of fizzy orange soda (my mother used Fanta)

A pinch of salt

## For the Filling:

$2\frac{1}{2}$ cups chopped black olives (washed and with pits removed)

2 medium-large onions finely chopped or grated

$\frac{1}{4}$ cup fresh mint leaves

$\frac{1}{4}$ cup fresh coriander leaves

$\frac{1}{4}$ cup spring onions (scallions), chopped

Lightly grease a baking pan and prepare oven by heating at medium temperature.
Sift flour with baking powder in a bowl; add salt. Slowly add olive oil to flour and knead. Begin adding the orange soda little by little until you have a fluffy dough.

Finely chop the fresh herbs and spring onions and combine with olives and chopped onion mixture. Set aside. Roll out the dough into small rounds (about 6 inches in diameter) like little pizzas and add the filling mixture. Roll the dough over the filling and gently shape into small round loaves. Place each loaf in pan until everything has been used up. Brush tops with olive oil.

Bake for about 35-45 minutes.

## GREEN LINE

I can't see this green line.
Textures are more useful,
like the crevice this finger traces around your masks
and the damp breath of those still alive
and the theatre of sighs,
as we post our condemnation to various presidents,
the acrid envelope's lip

and sometimes our little towns are quiet
and only flags flutter as tributes to the silence,

and I poke my tongue
into the hole of my history
and wriggle my toes in the damp sand, beyond the cafeteria,
and observe that I can't see this green line, I just can't see it.

I can only see gold,
and the eyes of my people blacker than embers,
and the strong smell of their lovemaking,
and secrets which they say nestle in their breasts,
standing like monoliths looking toward the sea,
saying nothing
they are chanting.

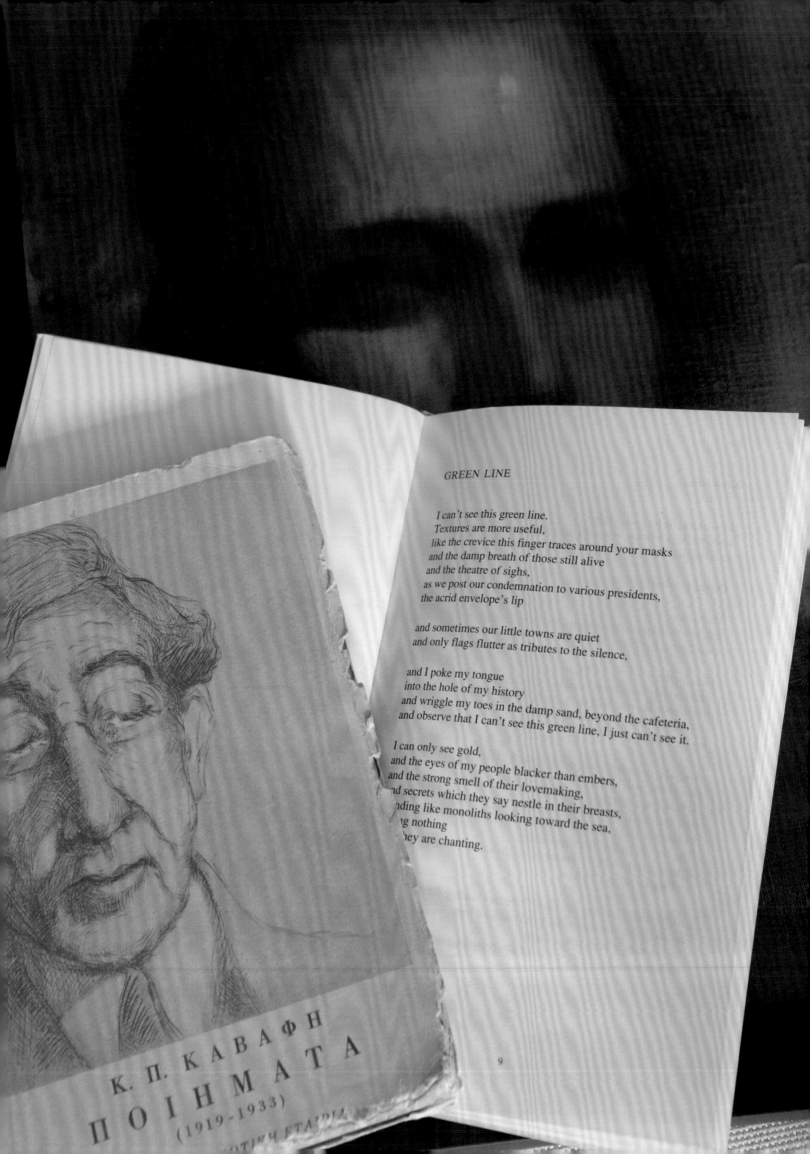

Κ. Π. ΚΑΒΑΦΗ
ΠΟΙΗΜΑΤΑ
(1919-1933)

## LYSANDROS PITHARAS TSANOS
## MY BELOVED BROTHER

Poet, singer, songwriter, international journalist, filmmaker, and political activist, Lysandros was a gorgeous baby who grew up to be a handsome and striking young man. He was three years younger than me and, as the first boy of the family, was named after my father's father—a great honor in a Cypriot household. Sandy lived life to the fullest. It was as if he somehow knew that his life was going to be cut short and wanted to do everything before his time was up. In his short 32 years of life, he managed to accomplish what most of us do not come close to achieving in the eight or nine decades that we may be fortunate enough to be given. He was admired by everyone. The most beautiful of women and the most handsome of men would always be by his side, and they would all inevitably fall in love with him. The documentary "The Story of the Rembetiko," which he wrote, produced, and starred in, was a moving film about the history of Greek blues music, which received national acclaim when it aired on British television. Sandy was also a great poet and songwriter who delighted in any opportunity to perform with his guitar in front of an audience. He would add music to his poems, improvising each time so that no

two performances were alike. His poetry was so special and well-received that in the late 1970s, his unique style was the subject of a BBC radio interview. I treasure a recording I have of Sandy in an impressive radio interview in which he recited his poem "I Am The 20th Century." He spoke with the same passion and energy about the Apartheid policy in South Africa, the cultural divide of Cyprus, the many questions raised by the sudden surge in HIV and AIDS, and the intricacies of his favorite jazz and blues pieces. He was as keen to share his opinions as he was to hear those of others. Following his death, a dear friend of both mine and Lysandros helped me to gather and publish a slim volume of his work. The messages he conveyed in his lyrics and poems were so poignant and forward-thinking that they still bear great relevance and beauty today, nearly twenty years later. As young children we never fought. My mother always said it was as if we knew we were going to lose each other early in life. He was my best friend and I shared all my secrets with him. Even though he was younger than me, his wisdom, compassion, spirit, and intellect guided me through my teenage years. I feel as though he has never left my side: He is still the keeper of my innermost thoughts and dreams. For Sandy, were he alive today, the first thing

I think I would cook is Cypriot ravioles. These are light pasta pockets filled with our favorite halloumi cheese and mint. We would often have them at home for Sunday lunch before the meat course. They are one of the most traditional dishes of Cyprus and truly represent the heritage of which my brother was so proud. When made at home, they require the same attention to detail that Sandy dedicated to everything he did. Oddly, they can be served as either a very elegant dish or as the most comforting meal, a rare combination.

OPPOSITE On the cover of the book is Constantine Cavafy, my brother's favorite Greek poet; Sandy taught me to adore him. He was greatly influenced by Cavafy's writing style. "Green Line" is a poem Sandy wrote about Cyprus.

ABOVE Sandy, center, was photographed with two of his colleagues at City Limits, a trendy London-based magazine that he worked on from its inception.

OVERLEAF RIGHT The handwritten letter was his last letter to me before he died in January of 1992, when he was 32.

# KYPRIAKES RAVIOLES — "CYPRIOT RAVIOLES"

## SERVES 4-6

**FOR DOUGH:**

1½ CUPS FLOUR

¼ CUP WATER

4 EGG YOLKS

1 TSP SALT

1 EGG FOR SEALING PASTA/
VEGETABLE OR CHICKEN STOCK
FOR BOILING FINISHED PASTA

**FOR FILLING:**

1½ CUP GRATED HALLOUMI CHEESE

3 EGG YOLKS

1 TBSP OF FRESH MINT, CHOPPED
(DRY MAY ALSO BE USED)

**FOR GARNISH:**

1 CUP OF GRATED HALLOUMI

1 TSP OF FRESH MINT
(DRY MAY ALSO BE USED)

SIFT FLOUR AND ADD THE SALT. MAKE A SMALL HOLLOW IN THE FLOUR, ADD THE EGGS INTO IT AND STIR. MOISTEN LITTLE BY LITTLE WITH COLD WATER AND KNEAD THE DOUGH UNTIL SMOOTH. ONCE SMOOTH, ROLL INTO BALL, COAT WITH A LITTLE OLIVE OIL AND WRAP WITH PLASTIC. DOUGH SHOULD REST LIKE THIS FOR 20-30 MINUTES BEFORE ROLLING OUT. PASS THE DOUGH THROUGH A MACHINE (IF AVAILABLE) OR ELSE ROLL OUT VERY THIN. CUT DOUGH INTO ROUND PIECES WITH THE BRIM OF A WINE GLASS.

WHILE THE DOUGH IS RESTING FOR THE 20-30 MINUTES, PREPARE THE FILLING BY MIXING THE THREE EGG YOLKS WITH THE HALLOUMI AND MINT.

PUT ONE TBSP OF THIS STUFFING INTO THE MIDDLE OF EACH PIECE OF DOUGH. BEAT THE LAST EGG IN A CUP, DIP A BRUSH IN THE EGG MIX AND COAT THE EDGE OF THE DOUGH THAT HAS ALREADY BEEN STUFFED. FOLD DOUGH AND PRESS THE EDGES LIGHTLY TOGETHER.

PUT CHICKEN OR VEGETABLE STOCK IN A SAUCEPAN TO BOIL, AND GENTLY PLACE THE RAVIOLES IN, ONE BY ONE. LEAVE THEM IN STOCK FOR ABOUT 8-10 MINUTES.

FINALLY, DRAIN THE WATER AND PLACE RAVIOLES ONTO A PLATTER, WHICH IS ALREADY SPRINKLED WITH GRATED HALLOUMI MIXED WITH THE MINT. SPRINKLE MORE OF THE HALLOUMI AND MINT ON TOP. SERVE HOT.

Baby brothers never stop being baby brothers, regardless of how old, tall, or grown-up they may become. George, *left,* is, and always will be, my baby brother. I am sure that anyone who has a little brother will understand my sentiment that baby brothers can really do no wrong. There is no limit to how much I want to spoil George—to the point that, I admit, I am sometimes looked at with raised eyebrows. As a grown-up, George loves the luxuries of life. Traveling and shopping are two of the things that we most look forward to doing together. That's when we are somehow transported back to our youth, when our father and brother, Sandy, were still alive and when we had fun every day. Life felt like one big adventure, and the whole family was in it together. The love of food is something George and I have shared from day one. His appreciation of a good meal is truly unparalleled. George does not simply talk about a meal, but rather describes an "experience." He has such a refined palette and innate sense of what is exceptional that he makes what some see as the mundane act of eating an intellectual and sensual journey. George can pinpoint every flavor and ingredient in a dish. He finds equal joy in a delicious plate of fish and chips from the local take-out as he does in an artfully presented filet mignon from a fancy restaurant in the West End of London. For him, it is all about the taste. It has always been such a pleasure to cook for and eat with George, and with him in mind, I am always encouraged to strive for excellence. Sunday lunches were always an event in our house and, as children, these simple-to-make and delicious roast potatoes were one of our favorites. But the best part of all was when Georgie—always my partner in crime—and I would sneak into the kitchen late Sunday night to eat the leftovers. I think Mum must have known that two little munchkins would appear every Sunday night, as there was always a full roasting pan magically awaiting our visit.

ABOVE LEFT George and I have a passion for traveling and seeing new places. He documents our trips by writing poems or keeping a journal while I enjoy taking photographs.

OPPOSITE To make George's potatoes, I parboil two-and-a-half pounds of peeled and washed yellow potatoes for five minutes, quarter them, and spread them in a baking dish. Then I add a large sliced onion, half a cup of extra virgin olive oil, the juice of two lemons, six to eight bay leaves, sea salt, and freshly-ground black pepper. Placing the dish on the middle rack of the oven, I cook the potatoes for about an hour at 350°F.

George's favourite
Greek Roast
Potatoes with
lemon and bay
leaves

A Cypriot wedding is never a minimal affair. Cypriot weddings can last anywhere from three days to an entire week, with each day marked by a different form of celebration. However, a modern wedding in Cyprus, although still filled with many festivities and traditions, is usually reduced to a single day. It is customary for the bride to get dressed at home while her family attends to her by singing, playing music, dancing, and eating. The groom prepares himself similarly in his own home, with his family members gathered around to observe. Before getting dressed, the groom traditionally undergoes a series of preparatory rituals. One such practice is the act of shaving. The groom sometimes receives a "final shave" from his best man, called the koumbaro, who shaves his groom's face clean as a symbol of his passage from boyhood to manhood, and his transition from an innocent youth to a responsible adult. The Greek Cypriot marriage ceremony is perhaps the longest I have ever witnessed, but also one of the most beautiful. The bride and groom wear wedding wreaths put together from pearls, gold, and flowers. These ornate wreaths are exchanged three times before being placed on the heads of the bridal couple to represent the holiness of their connection and their unique relationship. The wedding rings are also exchanged three times, a holy number representative of God, the Son, and the Holy Spirit. When the ceremony is over, the celebration truly begins. Rice is thrown at the newly married couple as they exit the church, and small wedding favors of sugarcoated almond sweets, called bomboniera, are passed out to the guests. At the reception, food, wine, and dance are in abundance. At one point, the guests gather to watch the bride and groom perform the "Choros Tou Androjinou," or the Dance of the Married Couple. This is also referred to as the money dance, because the guests take turns pinning notes onto the newly married couple. We would try to make the money train as long as possible so that the bride and groom could barely move. The money often serves as the wedding gift, intended to help the newlyweds begin their lives together as husband and wife.

Some of my first cousins' weddings that I have attended include Soulla and Costas', *opposite*, Sophie and Pavlos', *above left*—who are still crazy about dancing, to Greek music in particular—and George and Sharon's, *left*. She wanted a "winter wonderland" wedding. Her fur crown didn't hinder her from participating in the money dance.

PREVIOUS PAGES At Greek weddings, the wedding cake is usually served in between the dances. Sometimes, it is a confection covered in white roses, a symbol of innocence and purity. The tradition of the white rose is also rooted in Greek mythology, as it is said that when Aphrodite was born from the sea, a white foam formed around her figure. When the sea foam touched the earth, white roses appeared for the first time. This means that the shores of Cyprus not only gave birth to the most beautiful of goddesses, but also to the most beautiful of flowers. The hand-embroidered lace tablecloth—one of many such beautiful pieces—was given to me by my mother on my wedding day. I found some dove plates on my travels and thought they would be perfect on a wedding table or as a gift to the newlyweds. Even today, in Greek families, it is customary for a girl to be given a dowry. I was so excited when my daughters were born, as I knew that I could pass on to them all of the beautiful things I was given for my wedding.

LEFT Nuts are often served on special occasions as a sign of hospitality, or at weddings, where they symbolize fertility for the newlyweds.

OPPOSITE Bomboniera are sugar-coated almond treats that are traditionally given to all of the wedding guests as a small thank you. The nut bowls and silver spoons belonged to my family and were given to me when I married. Silver, lace, and hand embroidery are still very much part of the Cypriot household today. The filigreed design on the coffee spoons are an example of the fine work that has influenced both the textile and silver industries of Cyprus.

# KOURABIETHES (GREEK SHORTBREAD COOKIES)

MAKES BETWEEN 25-30 COOKIES

1 CUP UNSALTED BUTTER, MELTED
3 TABLESPOONS CONFECTIONERS' SUGAR, SIFTED (ICING SUGAR)
1 EGG YOLK
1 TBSP BRANDY
½ CUP FINELY CHOPPED ALMONDS
1½ CUP PLAIN FLOUR
1 TSP BAKING POWDER
2 CUPS OF CONFECTIONERS' SUGAR

PREHEAT OVEN TO 275°F. MELT BUTTER AND POUR INTO ELECTRIC MIXER. ADD SUGAR AND BEAT UNTIL LIGHT AND FLUFFY. ADD EGG YOLK AND BRANDY AND BEAT WELL.

REMOVE BOWL FROM MIXER AND ADD ALMONDS. SIFT FLOUR AND BAKING POWDER TWICE AND MIX LIGHTLY INTO BUTTER MIXTURE AND KNEAD BY HAND UNTIL SMOOTH.

BREAK OFF SMALL TABLESPOON-SIZE BITS AND SHAPE INTO BALLS OR HALF MOONS.

PLACE ON PARCHMENT AND BAKE FOR 20 MINUTES AT 325°F OR UNTIL LIGHT BROWN. LEAVE AND LET COOL. TAKE THE 2 CUPS OF CONFECTIONERS' SUGAR AND WHEN COOKIES ARE COMPLETELY COOLED, SIFT TOP AND SIDES.

THESE COOKIES ARE BEST LEFT IN A SEALED CONTAINER FOR A FEW DAYS TO BRING OUT THE FLAVOR.

# KATAIFI

Makes about 40 pieces

1lb Kataifi Pastry
1 Cup melted Butter

Nut Filling:
1 Cup Coarsely Ground Walnuts
1 Cup Coarsely Ground Almonds
½ Cup Caster Sugar
1 Tsp Ground Cinnamon
¼ Tsp Ground Cloves
1 Egg White, Lightly Beaten
1 Tbsp Brandy

Syrup:
2 Cups of Sugar
1½ Cups Water
1 Tsp Lemon Juice
Rind of 1 Lemon
4 Cloves
1 Piece Cinnamon Bark

First Step should be to preheat oven to 325°F. Then make nut filling by combining all the ingredients. Then take 1/8 of the pastry strands and spread out on a rectangular board (7 x 10 inches) with strands running roughly lengthwise. Using pastry brush, dab melted butter over pastry. Divide nut filling into 8 parts and spread filling along one edge. (The narrow edge).
Roll up into a neat roll. Repeat with remaining ingredients.

Bake in a moderate oven for 50-55 minutes or until golden brown.

Meanwhile, dissolve sugar in water over heat, add lemon juice, lemon rind, cloves and cinnamon.
Bring to boil and continue on medium heat for 10 minutes. Set aside and let cool.

Poor cooled syrup over hot pastries and place a folded cloth on top and leave to cool.

Cut into about 4-inch rolls.

# MELOMAKARONA - HONEY COOKIES WITH WALNUTS

MAKES BETWEEN 25-30 COOKIES

1 CUP SUGAR
1 CUP ORANGE JUICE
3 CUPS CORN OIL
½ CUP COGNAC
1 TBSP GROUND CINNAMON
1 TSP SALT
8½ CUPS FLOUR (APPROX)
5/6 TSP BAKING POWDER

SYRUP:
1½ CUPS SUGAR
    (USE CASTER OR VERY FINE SUGAR)
1½ CUPS WATER

NUT MIXTURE:
1 TBSP HONEY
2 CUPS FINELY CHOPPED WALNUTS
1 TSP GROUND CINNAMON
2 DROPS ALMOND ESSENCE

1 CUP OF COARSELY
CHOPPED ALMONDS FOR DECORATION
(OPTIONAL)

PRE HEAT OVEN 250°F - 275°F

IN A LARGE MIXING BOWL ADD SUGAR, ORANGE JUICE, OIL, COGNAC, CINNAMON, 7 CUPS OF FLOUR, BAKING POWDER AND SALT. MIX WELL BY HAND AND KEEP ADDING FLOUR LITTLE BY LITTLE UNTIL YOU ACHIEVE A NICE DOUGH (IT WILL FEEL A LITTLE OILY BUT THIS IS HOW IT SHOULD BE - IF TOO MUCH, ADD 1 MORE CUP OF FLOUR)

TAKE SMALL AMOUNT OF DOUGH MIXTURE AND MAKE INTO OVAL SHAPE. PLACE ONE BY ONE IN A BAKING TRAY WITH PARCHMENT AND COOK UNTIL THEY ARE ROSY BROWN, APPROX 30 MINUTES. ALLOW TO COOL WELL.

FOR NUT MIXTURE. PLACE ALL INGREDIENTS IN A BOWL AND MIX.

FOR SYRUP, HEAT SUGAR AND WATER, MIXING WITH A WOODEN SPOON, AND BRING TO BOIL.

ONCE THE SYRUP HAS COME TO A BOIL REMOVE FROM HEAT. TAKE THE COOKIES (WELL COOLED AT THIS POINT) AND, WITH A SLOTTED SPOON, PLACE THEM ONE BY ONE IN THE HEATED SYRUP FOR ABOUT 10-15 SECONDS OR UNTIL THEY ARE WELL SOAKED. LIFT OUT OF SYRUP WITH SLOTTED SPOON AND ROLL CAREFULLY IN THE NUT MIXTURE. KEEP THE SYRUP WARM AS YOU ARE DOING THIS BY REHEATING IT WHEN IT GETS COLD. CONTINUE UNTIL ALL COOKIES HAVE BEEN DIPPED AND ROLLED IN NUT MIXTURE.

YOU CAN SPRINKLE THE COARSELY CHOPPED ALMONDS ON EACH COOKIE FOR DECORATION.

The weaving and embroidering of textiles by women is a tradition on Cyprus that has been passed down through many generations. For such a small island, there is a remarkable amount of variation between the textiles that come from the different regions. One particularly stunning form of embroidery, called *Lefkarito* after its village of origin, Lefkara, was influenced by Venetian lace and was brought to Cyprus in the mid-fourteenth century. The technique is called "cutwork design," as it involves using one piece of plain linen or cotton and counting and cutting each individual thread so as to stitch a pattern into the background. Some of the more intricate and larger pieces can take months, or even a year, to complete. The techniques of making textiles such as Lefkarito have endured because of the incredible creativity, dexterity, and discipline of Cypriot women of the past and of today. Such skills have been handed down through the generations, as it was customary for mothers to teach them to their daughters—sometimes beginning when they were as young as eight years old—to prepare the raw materials, weave on the loom, and embroider. Throughout my life, I have been fortunate enough to have been given extraordinary textiles by my mother and my aunts. Knowing the history and tradition of these pieces, these gifts are very meaningful to me. I delight in using them in my home and in knowing that, one day, I will pass them on to my daughters.

LEFT The "Doves on Bridal Wreath" ceramic decoration is a symbol of peace, purity, and love.

OPPOSITE Myro Psara, a young ceramicist who has a workshop in Larnaca, the third largest city of Cyprus, created a beautiful collection of white earthenware pieces that would make perfect wedding gifts or festive table adornments. The artist's work is inspired by ancient Greek mythology. She uses motifs of laurel and olive branch wreaths and doves, which represent blessings for the newlyweds and the wish that their new home be filled with happiness and eternal love.

# 3: Arriving in America

Not in my wildest dreams did I ever imagine I would move to America. It seemed much too big and alien to ever think about making it my home. Then Andrew Sheinman came into my life and changed all that when he invited me to come to New York City with him in 1979, when both of us were still in our early twenties. We have never looked back. Living in New York has strongly awakened the "Greekness" and "Englishness" in me. I am so proud to have come from such strong cultural influences, and in America, I found the balance between them. In my New York, I go searching for that special spice in midtown, or I go on a trip to Astoria to buy my favorite olive oil or Cypriot cheese. I can walk into a diner, knowing that I can speak Greek and be understood. I have the luxury of being within walking distance from some of the best food markets, giving me numerous choices as to what I want to cook that evening for my family and friends. My house is also where the important traditional holidays are celebrated. Greek Easter still smells, tastes, and feels like it did all those years ago in my parents' home. Moving to the United States, I was worried about leaving behind my Cypriot and English backgrounds. I am so happy that I never had to do that.

OPPOSITE Astoria, a neighborhood in Queens, New York, is home to a very lively and large Greek and Cypriot population.

Greek Independence Day, when the country was freed from the 300-year Ottoman rule on March 25th, 1821, is celebrated every spring in New York with a week-long series of cultural activities that culminates in a parade in Manhattan. Participants from schools, churches, and philanthropic and political organizations march up Fifth Avenue to the delight of flag-waving and enthusiastic crowds. I always look forward to seeing the young school children dressed up in "tsolia," traditional folkloric costumes. While my daughters attended an after-school Greek program, learned all the traditional songs, and participated in the parade, they never consented to wearing the costumes.

PREVIOUS PAGES Whenever my family and I want to buy or eat something authentically Greek, we jump in the car and head to Astoria, Queens, where there is a large Greek community and, consequently, lots of Greek restaurants and stores. It is fun for us to wander around the area and listen to Greek being spoken while we eat a fresh spinach pie. I'm in heaven when I'm in Titan Foods, the largest supermarket in the area. The shop carries a huge selection of Greek foods and ingredients, not to mention an impressive feta cheese counter. I often get nostalgic recognizing the old labels and packaging that take me back to my childhood—whether in Green Lanes in North London, at the Monastiraki market in Athens, or in Charalambides, in Cyprus.

Before coming to the United States, the only image I had of the quintessential American diner was the one I had seen in movies—packed with high school students drinking thick milkshakes and eating juicy hamburgers. I couldn't wait to see this American scene for myself. Having now lived in New York for over 30 years, I know how different the reality is. What I thought to be totally American is actually more closely tied to Greek culture, as many diners in New York are owned by people of Greek or Cypriot descent. While I recognized the long counters and stools and the booths with their Formica-topped tables, I was surprised to see the huge menus that included pages of "Greek specialties" like chicken souvlaki, moussaka, and spanakopita, or spinach pies. I also discovered that coffee in most of the New York diners is supplied by the Greek Vassilaros family. "Vassilaros coffee has been filling New York's Coffee Cup since 1919" is the slogan that can be seen on the company's trucks as they deliver coffee to local luncheonettes and restaurants. The Greeks have such a strong influence in the diner industry that the paper blue-and-white take-out coffee cup, often decorated with a Greek key motif and drawings of Greek vases, is ubiquitous. It is also such an iconic object that a company called "We Are Happy To Serve You" has made a ceramic version, *above right*, which is sold in the Museum of Modern Art gift shops, along with other objects of classic modern design.

Two of my favorite Greek cheeses are feta, *opposite,* and kefalotyri, *right,* both of which are made from a blend of sheep and goats' milk. Feta is salty, soft, and crumbly, while kefalotyri is hard and somewhat sharp. Both are delicious in salads, grilled (called saganaki), or just eaten plain with a slice of bread. A blend of the two is a staple of the Greek kitchen as the filling for the phyllo-dough–based spinach spanakopita or cheese tiropita pies. A warm and buttery cheese pie that has just come out of the oven is what I call my ultimate comfort food.

It was very important for me to have my two daughters, Alexia Valentina Sheinman and Isabel Anastasia Sheinman, grow up with an understanding of and a connection to their Greek Cypriot heritage. From the beginning I was raised with two cultures—I was both Greek and British. As a young girl, it made me feel unique to have this blend in my life, and it made me see the world as a much larger place. I developed the ability to balance both value systems, jumping from one to the other at any given moment. This was my hope for my daughters. I decided that the best way to accomplish this was through food, as I believe that appreciating the smells and tastes of a nation's food opens the door to understanding its traditions and values. It is my hope that this understanding sparks an interest in further exploring the music, dance, and language, and other aspects of that society. I really do believe that through food, you can immerse yourself in a different culture. Once you learn to engage with a culture other than your own, it follows naturally that you become more attuned to others. Getting the girls to learn Greek was, at first, a tricky task, as they dreaded their afterschool Greek classes and had nobody besides me to practice with. When my mother, Agnes, came to live with us in New York for several years—following the sudden death of my father in 1992—it became far easier to teach the girls, as she insisted on speaking to them only in Greek. Alexia and Isabel both read, write, and speak Greek very well now, and are grateful that we persisted in spite of their protests. With my mother and I together in New York, the girls grew to love being in the kitchen. Their grandmother made any time they spent by her side fun and playful, and there was never a day that they were not learning something new. We began making olive and cheese breads and the traditional "S" cookies with them when they were still very young. My mother quickly became a

grandmother to so many others in New York. Alexia and Isabel's friends and teachers alike would call her Yia Yia, as they grew to love her like a member of their own family. She was constantly in and out of the classroom from pre-K to second grade, sharing that same joy of cooking and baking not just with her granddaughters, but with all the other children. To this day, some 20 years later, these same children (now young adults) still refer to my mother as Yia Yia. At a very early age, the girls learned to eat such things as homemade tzatziki, yoghurt with mint and cucumber, *opposite left,* and hummus, a mixture of chickpeas, tahini, and lots of lemon juice, *opposite far left,* which we would add to vegetables or put in a sandwich. To my joy, once their taste buds grew acclimated to these flavors, there wasn't anything I cooked that they wouldn't eat. To my even greater delight, as they grew older, not only did Alexia and Isabel learn to eat a wide array of foods, but they also became interested in cooking themselves and, as I had hoped, had no fear of being in the kitchen. It made me so happy to watch the ease and playfulness with which they approached cooking, never afraid to experiment with different ingredients. I remembered how my life had grown richer and more satisfying once I had awakened my taste buds, and I could already see this change in my girls.

OPPOSITE These wonderful handmade bowls and platter were crafted by Yiannos Anastasiou, who lives in Limassol, Cyprus.

RIGHT Alexia, *far right,* is two years older than her sister Isabel. The two girls have always been best friends.

# Kritharaki (Greek Orzo) with Shiitake Mushrooms and Pesto

For Alexia, Isabel and all their friends...... It has been such a pleasure to cook this dish over and over again as per your requests.

3 cups Kritharaki
2 cups Shiitake mushrooms or mixed blend
Pesto (see recipe, below)
Pine Nuts
Asparagus Tips
Grated Halloumi & Parmesan Cheese

For Pesto:
2 cups Basil Leaves (washed well)
2 cups Spinach (washed well)
$\frac{1}{4}$ Cup Toasted Pine Nuts
2 cups Olive Oil
$\frac{1}{4}$ Cup Grated Halloumi and $\frac{1}{4}$ cup Parmesan, Combined
Salt/Pepper

Preparation For Pesto:
Take Basil and Spinach leaves and put into Cuisinart. Pulse Gently, adding Toasted Pine Nuts, grated cheese, salt and pepper. Drizzle the Olive Oil while pulsing (I like to make pesto chunkier) to desired consistency.

Method:
In a separate deep frying pan add mushrooms with some Olive Oil. Sauté until they are soft. Add Asparagus tips and Sauté for 3-5 minutes more. Add salt & pepper.

Boil water in another large saucepan with 2 bay leaves and a drop of olive oil.

Once water is boiling, add orzo and cook until al dente (approx 15-20 minutes). Drain water and add a little of the grated cheese to the orzo.

Place orzo in a nice serving dish and add pesto, followed by the mushrooms with asparagus. Carefully mix all ingredients together and serve with the remainder of the grated cheese on top.

Shelter Island, located at the tip of Long Island, New York, is our escape from the noise and speed of city life. The seven-minute ferry ride—the last leg of the journey out there—makes us feel as though we are already miles and miles away from our everyday routines. Andrew and I were married there in 1986 on the grounds of the Ram's Head Inn. We had arrived in New York a few years prior, hoping to make a new beginning for ourselves in America. Shelter Island became "our island" from the very first day we stepped off the ferry, and I knew it was where I wanted to have my wedding. June 29th, 1986, was truly an idyllic day. Members from both sides of our families came from London and stayed at the inn with us a few days before the event—helping us wrap the trees with huge white organza bows and paint ceramic pots filled with white hydrangeas for the centerpieces of each table. We had an English-style high tea on the lawn in the afternoon, and Greek and American dancing on the porches after dinner. Andrew, an interior designer, and Demetris Doupis, an architect, designed and built our beautiful Greek Revival house on the island. Andrew also designed a kitchen with a large center island, industrial appliances, and plenty of storage, *opposite*, making it easy and enjoyable for me to cook for large numbers of people who sit around our vintage dining table, *opposite, bottom left*.

RIGHT During the summer we love to combine mozzarella with delicious local tomatoes and fresh basil from our garden. We call it our Shelter Island version of Greek salad.

OVERLEAF The beautiful and functional back porch, with its retractable awning, looks onto Crab Creek, and can seat up to 30 people—rain or shine.

My husband, Andrew, trans-
formed an ordinary ranch
house into a classically
elegant two-story crisp white
house with thick columns
and a wide front porch, *left,*
and a spacious living room
focused on a brick-lined
fireplace, *opposite.*

Easter is one of the most celebrated and important holidays on the Greek Orthodox calendar. It is a time of renewal, and a time to reflect on one's values and family obligations. Houses are cleaned and painted so they sparkle, and many people buy something new to wear. When our daughters were younger I would always make a point to celebrate it. We would attend services at the Greek Orthodox Cathedral of the Holy Trinity in Manhattan on Good Friday, and have a special lunch on Easter Sunday. One of the traditional things to bake during this time are the Easter flaounes, or cheese breads. Flaounes are a Cypriot specialty made only at this time of the year. These breads are made with a mixture of cheeses, including halloumi, kaskavali, and kefalotyri. The addition of mint adds a sweetness to the filling. The dough is rolled very thinly and sesame seeds are added to the outside for more taste and to give the dough a festive look. Those who have observed Lent and have not eaten meat or dairy foods for 40 days break their fast on Easter Sunday. The focus of the day is how to cook the perfect leg of lamb—either roasted or cooked souvlaki-style—as large pieces of meat cooked on a long spit and rotated slowly over a charcoal barbecue. Each household has their own special dishes to accompany it. In our family's home in London, we always had avgolemono soup, a traditional egg-lemon soup, the lamb with roasted artichokes and potatoes, and a semolina orange cake. These are all dishes that I have continued to make every year in America. Celebrating Easter like this in New York transports me back to the familiar smells and tastes of my mother's kitchen in London.

RIGHT The large colorful basket, known as tsetsos, is used at Easter to hold flaounes, special breads, and cheese pies. The pottery head is by Anna Antonopoulou.

# Greek Easter Bread

Makes one loaf

Ingredients:

10 grams Active dry yeast
½ cup of warm milk
6 cups of white flour
2 eggs, beaten
½ tsp of caraway seeds
1 tbsp caster sugar (superfine)
1 tbsp brandy
1 cup orange juice
2 tbsp orange zest
¼ cup melted butter
1 egg white, beaten
1 egg, dyed red
1 tsp of salt, mixed in with the flour
½ cup of sliced almonds (optional)

Method:

Crumble the yeast into a bowl. Mix with 2 tbsp warm water until softened. Add the milk and one cup of the flour and mix until you get a loose dough consistency. Cover with cloth and leave in a warm place to rise for one hour.

Stir remaining flour into a large bowl and make a well in the center. Pour the risen yeast into the well, add the eggs, caraway seeds, sugar, O.J., zest and brandy. Now make a dough

Mix in the melted butter. Turn onto a floured surface and knead until the dough becomes smooth.
Return to bowl and cover with cloth.
Leave in warm place for about 3 hours.

Preheat oven to 350° F. Punch down dough and knead on a floured surface for a minute or two. Divide into three and roll each piece into a long roll. Make a braid about 18 inches long with the three pieces. Place the bread onto a greased baking sheet.

Brush with the egg white and decorate with the dyed egg. Add almonds (optional).

Bake for about one hour and serve hot or cold.

# Avgolemono Soup (Egg Lemon Soup)

Serves 4-6

Ingredients:
- 3¾ cups of chicken stock
- 1½ cup of long grain rice
- 3 egg yolks
- Juice of two lemons
- Salt/pepper to taste
- Lemon slices as garnish (optional)

Pour stock into a saucepan and bring to a simmer. Add the rice and cook until just tender.

Whisk the egg yolks in a bowl and add the lemon juice, a little at a time, whisking constantly until the mixture is smooth. Now add 1 cup of broth from the pan, a little at a time, to the lemon and egg mixture, whisking constantly. Then pour the egg mixture back into the soup and stir. The soup will turn a pretty lemon color and will thicken slightly. Add salt & pepper and serve hot in bowls.

This soup is traditionally served with boiled chicken. I have served it with shellfish and drizzled olive oil on top, which is a delicious alternative.

# Pourgouri — Bulgur Pilaf

Ingredients:

1 medium-size onion, finely chopped
½ cup of olive oil
3¼ cup of chicken stock or water
2 cups of coarse bulgur
1 cup of vermicelli pasta
3 cinnamon sticks
Yoghurt (preferably Greek) for dressing
Salt/Pepper to taste.

Place chicken stock/water in saucepan and heat. In a deep pan gently saute onion until transparent. Add cinnamon sticks and continue to saute. Meanwhile break vermicelli into small pieces and bake in moderate oven until brown. (Watch carefully as it browns quickly).

Place bulghur in a sieve and rinse quickly under cold water. Add to onion. Add vermicelli, salt/pepper and water/stock. Bring to light boil. Reduce heat and simmer gently until liquid is absorbed.

Remove pan from heat. Place cloth over rim of pan and replace lid. Leave for 15 minutes.

This is absolutely delicious served with thick Greek yoghurt.

# WHOLE ROAST LEG OF LAMB.

ONE OF MY FAMILY'S FAVOURITE SIDE DISHES
TO EAT WITH ROAST LAMB IS ARTICHOKES
WITH ROAST POTATOES.

4½lb leg of lamb
4-5 Pototoes
5-6 Garlic cloves, peeled and quartered lengthwise
Juice of 3 lemons
3 onions
2 cups Extra Virgin Olive Oil
Fresh Ground Pepper
Rosemary Sprigs
Sea Salt

HEAT TO VERY HOT OVEN (475° F).

WASH POTATOES AND QUARTER. THINLY SLICE ONIONS. PLACE
IN BOTTOM OF LARGE ROASTING PAN.
WASH AND PAT DRY LEG OF LAMB AND PLACE IN ROASTING
PAN OVER THE ONIONS AND POTATOES.
SPREAD OIL AND SEA SALT ALL OVER LAMB. PIERCE LAMB IN
VARIOUS PLACES, PRESSING THE POINT OF A SHARP KNIFE
DEEP INTO THE FLESH, AND INSERT GARLIC CLOVES AND
ROSEMARY SPRIGS. POUR LEMON JUICE ALL OVER THE MEAT
AND ADD ½ CUP OF WATER TO PAN.

ROAST LAMB FOR 15 MINUTES ON HIGH HEAT, TURNING
ALL AROUND SO IT BECOMES A NICE-LOOKING ROAST.
REDUCE HEAT TO 375° F AND ROAST FOR AN ADDITIONAL
1½ HOURS, BASTING AT LEAST FOUR TIMES. THEN TURN
OVER AND COOK FOR ANOTHER 30 MINUTES, BASTING
THREE TIMES.

LET THE MEAT REST FOR AT LEAST 10 MINUTES
BEFORE SERVING.

# Orange & Hazelnut Semolina Cake
## with Orange Syrup

For the Cake:

½ Cup of unsalted butter, softened
3 Eggs
½ Cup of Caster Sugar (superfine)
Finely Grated orange rind of one orange
½ Cup of orange juice at Room Temperature
1 Cup Semolina Flour
2 Tsp Baking Powder, sifted
1 Cup of Ground Hazelnuts (should have the consistency of flour - leave approx 10 whole)

For the Syrup:

1½ Cups of Caster Sugar (superfine)
2 Cinnamon Sticks
Juice of 1 Lemon
4 Tbsp of Orange Flower Water
Round, Finely sliced orange slices

Preheat oven to 425°F.
Grease the base and sides of
a 9-inch square deep cake pan.

Lightly cream Butter in a Bowl. Add the Sugar, orange rind and juice, eggs, Semolina, Baking Powder and hazelnuts, and beat the ingredients until smooth.

Put mixture into prepared cake pan and level the surface.

Bake for about 20-25 minutes until firm and golden. Allow to cool in the tin.

To make Syrup:

Put Caster Sugar in a small heavy pan with 2 cups of water and the Cinnamon Sticks. Heat gently over low heat, stirring frequently but carefully. Continue until all sugar has dissolved. Bring to a fast boil. Switch off. Measure half the syrup and add lemon juice and orange water to it. Pour this over the cake.

Leave cake in tin until syrup is absorbed and completely cool and then turn onto a plate.

Take a few of the orange slices and gently place them in pan with reserved syrup. Heat until the orange rinds become a nice caramel color, about 15 minutes. Remove from pan carefully as they are delicate. Place on top of the cake.

Now heat some hazelnuts in a pan with a small amount of the syrup. Once they begin to brown, remove and drizzle on cake.

# 4: CELEBRATING IN SERIFOS

Serifos is one of the smaller western Cycladic islands, located south of Kythnos and Sifnos. Because tourism has not been highly developed there, the island retains much of its authenticity and old world charm. On the island are white-washed houses with colorful shutters, narrow winding streets, 365 chapels (one for every day of the year), and many pristine beaches. The Hora, or town at the top of the hill, is considered one of the most beautiful capitals in the Cyclades. Years ago, iron mining played a major role in the island's economy, as the soil was rich in ore and mineral deposits. During the Venetian rule, Serifos flourished commercially because of the presence of these natural resources. After the mines closed in the 1960s, the island became deserted as the men sought work elsewhere. In the last 40 years, Serifos has been brought back to life by Greek families returning to claim their ancestral homes, and foreigners recognizing the appeal of an island that seems untouched by time. Some 15 years ago, as I was preparing to stay on the island for the first time, I called a friend to ask if we should bring tennis rackets and water skis with us. She explained that there were no hotels, organized activities, or modern-day luxuries—just dusty roads, basic plumbing, and simple electricity. I realized we were in for an adventure. My children learned to craft mosaics like the ancient Greeks, chipping colored glass and bits of tile, and making glue from fish bones. They learned to play backgammon and they ran through the town square with other children their age. Serifos is where we learned to pick fresh capers from the side of the path; it is where we learned to recognize the constellations and watch for shooting stars. But above all, Serifos is where we learned to simply relax—in the historic square of the Hora, in the tavernas at the port, or in Kyria Chrisoulla's café, one of the oldest on the island, where the same people have been sitting together for decades. Life just slows down there, especially for those who spend the rest of the year living in fast-paced cities. Serifos is a place that has given my family the invaluable opportunity to take a long, deep breath and realize how lucky we are to be together.

OPPOSITE An antique map shows Serifos as "Serpho," in the Cycladic group of islands.

OVERLEAF A 1950s postcard of Serifos depicts the island before it became developed.

PREVIOUS PAGES Hora, the mountain top capital of Serifos, is the epitome of traditional Greek island architecture. White-washed houses are clustered together and the village is accessible only by foot.

When we first came to Serifos, we rented a house at the highest point of the hill, called the Kastro, or castle, *previous pages*, named for its historically strategic military position. To get there, one drives up the mountain, parks the car, and then walks up about 250 stone steps through narrow, winding streets. The front of our house faced a massive rock—the same rock where, according to legend, the head of Medusa is buried. From the minute I saw the little house perched near the top of the hill, I knew it would make a perfect home. I now call this house "my diamond in the sky," *right*. I've always believed that if there is an ounce of creativity in anyone, it will be discovered after spending time on Serifos. There is something so inspiring about sitting on our Romeo and Juliet balcony, with its wide view of the harbor and all the sailboats. It is a rather surreal experience to sit so high up in the sky, eating watermelon or sipping Greek coffee, and watch the world unfold below. The interior of the house, *overleaf*, was renovated and decorated by Vassilis Tseghis, an Athenian architect who had the know-how and patience to convert some abandoned ruins into livable homes. Our house is in the Neoclassical style and has two rooms on each of its three levels. The original floor is in a pattern of black-and-white mosaic tile, and the ceilings are of beams constructed from wooden crossbars. The top bedroom opens to a tiny staircase that leads up to the roof. The kitchen just about fits a sink, refrigerator, and a small electric stove. Although tiny, the house worked perfectly for our young family. Over the years, we have managed to cook for as many as 30 people at parties out of our little kitchenette.

- ΓΛΥΚΟ ΣΑΛΑΜΑΚΙ (ΚΟΡΜΟΣ)
- ΚΕΪΚ ΣΟΚΟΛΑΤΑ
- ΚΑΡΥΔΟΠΙΤΑ
- ΧΑΛΒΑΣ ΣΙΜΙΓΔΑΛΕΝΙΟΣ
- ΑΧΛΑΔΙΑ ΣΤΟ ΚΡΑΣΙ
- Sweet Salami
- chocolate cake
- Walnut cake
- Khalvas
- Pears in wine

The main town square of Hora, or Pano Plateia, *opposite*, as it is known by the locals, is the ideal place to come to sit and recover after a steep climb up some 100 steps from the bus stop, as the village is built on the side of a mountain overlooking the harbor. This beautiful square houses the 17th century church of Agios Athanasios and the Neoclassical Town Hall building. There are also several small tavernas or restaurants, but our favorite is the café known as Stou Stratou, which simply means, At Stratos'. The owner, Stratos Mastorakis, is a special friend. Born in Athens, he has lived and studied in Paris and speaks many languages, including French, German, English and, of course, Greek. His café attracts many people during the April to October season, both visitors and locals alike. Everyone comes to sit and enjoy fresh peach or watermelon juice, or savor some of the specialties of the house, such as the walnut cake, the sweet salami cake, or his famous chocolate cake, *left*. At night, and even into the early hours of the morning, people are still scrambling to find a chair to perch on and become part of this picturesque and romantic "Serifiotiko" scene. Stratos has managed to create a very special gathering spot on Serifos. I look forward to going to the square every day when I am on the island, as I will inevitably run into someone I know—or meet someone new and interesting to talk with.

OVERLEAF LEFT Stratos, the owner of the café Stou Stratou, one of the most popular of the restaurants in the Hora, is famous for his chocolate cake.

OVERLEAF RIGHT A new addition to the café, once the ground floor of one of the small houses on the square, offers a place of refuge from the sun or the strong, sudden Meltemi winds of August. There is always good conversation and great music, which makes it easy to let hours drift by.

112

# Stratos' Chocolate Cake

As a chocolate addict, I must admit that this is my absolute favorite cake, especially when it comes straight out of the oven and is oozing warm chocolate. I am thrilled that Stratos shared his well-kept secret recipe with me. It only took eating the cake nearly every day for the past 15 summers - and gaining quite a few extra pounds in doing so - to gain his trust.


6 eggs
250 Grams margarine
250 Grams dark, good-quality chocolate
1 Cup Sugar
2 Cups Self-rising flour


Use Bundt Cake Mold. Set oven to 475° F.


Put Butter and Chocolate in a pan and melt. In a separate bowl, crack the eggs, add the sugar and mix. Add the butter and chocolate mixture and whisk together.

Grease the baking tin and then coat in flour so the cake releases easily.

Cook for approximately 13 minutes, depending on the oven. As soon as you see the first crack in the cake, it is ready.

Serve when completely cool.

PREVIOUS PAGES My friend Maritza Chateau captured the essence of Greek island architecture in this photograph.

In order to pay your electrical bill on Serifos, it is necessary to go to the electrical plant, which is located along a dusty, unpaved backroad just before you arrive at the port. I have been doing this for years, so you can imagine my utter delight when one day, by mistake, I drove past the plant and found myself at what seemed a dead end, only to discover a small driveway leading up to a farmhouse surrounded by goats, chickens, pigs, a donkey, and a variety of fruit and olive trees. That's how I first came across a hidden treasure that is simply known as Rita's. My curiosity was awakened as I timidly walked up to the front door of the house to see if anyone was there. A portly Greek man answered the door and introduced himself as Kyrie Giorgos—everyone in Greece is referred to by the polite form of Kyrie, mister, or Kyria, Mrs., followed by the person's first name. Kyrie Giorgos welcomed me by offering me samples of the delicacies, like rice pudding, orange cake, breads, and cheeses. I was thrilled to have discovered a new shop after years of thinking that I knew every corner of the island.

LEFT Kyria Rita stands in the doorway of her shop holding a tray of her special orange cake. She won't give away the recipe, but a piece of her cake—or her rice pudding—is the most delicious treat after a day of swimming and sunbathing.

OPPOSITE Having high tea at four o'clock in the afternoon is a ritual we never break in our family—no matter where we are in the world. I know a lot of my friends think it a little strange, but I always pack my own PG Tips tea bags wherever I go because nothing else tastes quite the same. Teatime on Serifos is even more special, as we accompany it with the orange cake that Kyria Rita made that morning.

LEFT I still recall my surprise as I walked into the air-conditioned, pristine, white-tiled shop. The shelves, stocked with bottles of olive oil, and jars of marmalade and capers, were a stark contrast to the smells and messiness of the animals that I had just seen outside. Each jar and bottle was so carefully placed and labeled that I immediately sensed that this shop was set up with meticulous care and attention to detail. I explained to Kyrie Giorgos that I was a Cypriot born in London, now living in New York, and that I loved food and cooking. After tasting some of his delicious cheeses and capers, I understood that everything there was homemade, bottled, or canned in the back room. I asked if I could take a peek. Kyrie Giorgos, his wife, Kyria Rita, and I began to chat about our passion for food. She had been a distinguished cook, not only on the island but throughout Greece, and had won a national prize for her cooking. She had written a cookbook. She explained that, wanting a simpler life, she now enjoys making only special things—her sundried tomatoes, marmalades, the Greek spoon sweets called glyka, cheeses, and, of course, her famous orange cake. It was only after we exchanged food stories that they invited me to take a look at the back of the store. Next to the kitchen was a room that housed shelf after shelf of Kyria Rita's special cheeses. I am such a cheese lover that I could never get tired of standing in a room surrounded by the delicious smell of fresh cheese while Kyria Rita explained when certain ones had been made and which ones would be ready in the near future. Many residents of Serifos put their orders in months before to guarantee that their favorite cheeses would be ready when they wanted them. Now I, too, always call ahead to place an order for two or three large cheeses to be ready for when we are all on Serifos.

OPPOSITE One of Kyria Rita's and Kyrie Giorgos' flock of French goats from Roquefort.

# Spinach Pie

On Serifos we refer to Sophia as the "Bougatsa Lady". Bougatsa is a traditional breakfast pastry made of thin sheets of phyllo dough (phyllo in greek means leaf) that can be filled with either spinach, cheese, minced meat, chicken, zucchini or, what I love after a long night of dancing, custard that is served warm and dusted with confectioners' sugar and cinnamon. The pies are made fresh every day, and it is not unusual to find a line of people waiting outside the bougatsa shop early in the morning. My special all-time favorite is the spinach, fennel and feta pie.

1 lb  Spinach (washed well)
1     Bunch parsley
1     Bunch mint
2     Bunches Spring Onions
½     Fennel Bulb
3     Eggs
½     Cup Olive Oil
1     Phyllo Dough (Packet)
1½    Cup of butter
1 lb  Feta Cheese
1 ts  nutmeg
Salt / Pepper

Preheat oven to 275°F

Finely chop the parsley & mint. Heat oil in saucepan and finely chop onions and fennel, and then add to oil. Saute until tender and then add parsley and mint until lightly coated.

Add spinach until wilted. Remove from heat.
Beat eggs in a bowl and mash the feta cheese in another.
Add both to spinach mixture. Add salt, pepper and nutmeg.
Melt butter and take one phyllo sheet at a time and lightly brush with melted butter. Place in ovenproof dish. Continue until you have completed half the dough. Spread filling on top, leaving sides clear. Continue to lightly butter the remaining dough and place on top of the filling. Fold in the sides to secure. Brush lightly with butter.
Bake for 25 minutes or until golden brown.

Serifos is known, above all, for beautiful and quiet beaches that have absolutely nothing on or around them other than the sea, sand, and, if you are lucky, the occasional tree for shade. The beach of Psili Ammos (from the Greek "psili," meaning soft, and "amos," sand) is probably the most popular on the island, in part because of its unique Manolis Taverna, which serves some of the best food on the entire island. While sipping a refreshing cold beer one can enjoy the delicious fava beans, fried calamari, Greek salad, and grilled octopus prepared by Manolis, *opposite,* his wife, Maria, their daughter, Eleni, her husband Andreas, and their two sons, Manolis and Yorgos. This family has owned the taverna for as long as anyone can remember. In August, not a minute goes by before an empty table is scooped up— there is a constant flow of customers and food from morning to evening. When we arrive for our first swim of the summer, Manolis welcomes us with open arms, and Maria insists on taking me into the kitchen, past the grape arbor, *left,* to see the special dishes of the day.

FRIED CALAMARI

½ LB SQUID
FLOUR
CORN OIL

METHOD:
WASH THE SQUID AND PLACE IN COLANDER
UNTIL THOROUGHLY DRY. SPRINKLE WITH SALT AND
DREDGE IN FLOUR AND FRY IN PLENTY OF
CORN OIL FOR 2 MINUTES.

REMEMBER TO KEEP HEAT HIGH.

SERVE WITH GREEK SALAD AND FRENCH
FRIES. YUMMY!!

PREVIOUS PAGES One of my favorite photographs is this one, taken by my daughter Alexia, of the lower terrace of our new house in the Karavi beach area of Serifos. It captures the dramatic setting. I love having dinner out there, at the ocean's edge, looking out onto the vastness of the Aegean Sea.

LEFT Kayaking off the beach below our house is an activity we all enjoy. We keep the kayaks on the beach so they are easy to access. We often use them to visit different bays along the coastline.

OPPOSITE Some of our guests seem never to move from the banquettes of our outside dining room. This porch is the perfect place to sit and read, nap, or just stare out at the ocean, as it is always protected from the strong sun and wind of summer on a Greek island.

OPPOSITE The beach house, which we bought after spending quite a number of years on Serifos, has a different feeling than our first house that was located at the top of the hora, or village. The high ceilings with their wooden beams are one of the house's special features.

ABOVE The rooms are much more spacious and comfortable, allowing both adults and children to play games in the living room. I adore the large windows that look out to the sea.

ALEXIA

2·1

PREVIOUS PAGES The terrace of our home was the perfect setting for a party that celebrated our daughter Alexia's 21st birthday.

OPPOSITE Alexia turned 21 the same year she graduated from the university of Bristol in England—both wonderful excuses to have a party. We decided on a sit-down dinner, and her father, Andrew, had the lovely idea of having napkins printed in New York. Each guest's name was written on a stone from our beach to serve as place cards.

RIGHT We set up one long table with enough room for 45 guests and made centerpieces out of small glass vases filled with basil, which not only looked pretty but gave off a lovely aroma throughout the evening. We served a combination of home-cooked dishes as well as the specialties of many of our favorite restaurants on the island, such as roasted lamb with potatoes, zucchini and fennel fritters, calamari, and meatballs. It was a true Greek feast and the beautiful sunset of that August evening added to its magic.

# FAMILY ALBUM

MY COUSIN GINA - HER BEAUTIFUL SMILE AND SUNNY DISPOSITION HAVE BEEN A CONSTANT SOURCE OF INSPIRATION TO ALL OF US.

THE BOYS: DEMETRIOS, MAX, ALEX, EMILIOS & SEAN (ALEXIA & LILY PEEKING THROUGH THE WINDOWS)

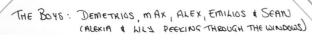

EMILIOS - OUR MUSICIAN & POET, WHO REMINDS ME IN MANY WAYS OF MY OWN BROTHER, LYSANDROS.

ELYSSIA & LILIA - MY TWO GREEK GODDESSES

ISABEL WITH NATALIE - FROM THE AGE OF FIVE THEY HAVE BEEN LIKE "TWO PEAS IN A POD" TOTALLY INSEPARABLE

ISABEL & ELIZABETH - AS FREE SPIRITED AS EVER.

ME, ALEX & ISABEL - OUR SPECIAL PASSION FOR PHILOSOPHY AND DEBATE HAS ALWAYS BOUND THE THREE OF US TOGETHER.

MY IZZY.
FOREVER WITH HER BIG SMILE AND APPETITE
TO GO WITH IT!

PHOEBE & IZZY - BOTH GROWING UP SO BEAUTIFULLY TOGETHER

RELAXING AT HOME
WITH MUM & GEORGE

HERE THEY ALL ARE: MY KIDS. EACH YEAR WE NEVER KNOW
WHAT WILL HAPPEN WHEN WE ARE TOGETHER ... BUT SOMETHING
MEMORABLE ALWAYS DOES.

ALEXIA, MY ANGEL & ROCK - LOOKING AS SHE ALWAYS
DOES, SERENE AND RADIANT.

OVERLEAF Nothing makes me happier than
having the opportunity to bring people together
to enjoy each other's company. Our friends,
young and old alike, who visit Serifos always
seem to discover a renewed appetite for life.

# CATALOG

Agapi is developing an artisanal product line that supports a community of artists rooted in Cyprus. All of the handicrafts incorporate traditional artisanal skills combined with modern design elements to provide a fresh translation of Cypriot cultural history.

Gelasto Collection
Set of 5 ceramic bowls
D 7 inches
Dishwasher safe
Artist: Kikis Pantehis Studio

Aegean Collection
Hand-painted stoneware
Source: Cyprus Handicraft Center

Antheia Plate
Stoneware with ruffle border
D 14 inches
Artist: Oria Petropoulou

Psari Collection
Earthenware bowls, dinner
and soup plates
D 13, 10 and 8 inches
Dishwasher safe
Artist: Myro Psara

Organic Collection
Stoneware uneven shape plate
with inlay design
Dishwasher safe
Artist: Oria Petropoulou

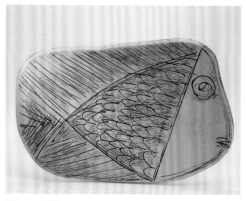

Nereus Platter
Stoneware
Available in various sizes
Artist: Efthymios Symeou

Dove Collection
Earthenware bowl
Large D 10 ½ inches
Dishwasher safe
Artist: Myro Psara

Artemis Bowl
Glazed earthenware fruit bowl,
hand-painted
H 6 inches x D 10 inches
Dishwasher safe
Artist: Kikis Pantehis Studio

Telete Collection
Large stoneware bowl
D 11 ½ inches
Dishwasher safe
Artist: Efthymios Symeou

# CATALOG

Many of the bowls, plates, and textiles featured in this book are part of our Agapi collection.  Please refer to our website, www.Agapistyle.com.

Lenaia Collection
Stoneware bowls
Large D 11 ½ inches; small D 9 inches
Dishwasher safe
Artist: Efthymios Symeou

Themele Collection
Earthenware soup bowl
D 9 ½ inches
Artist : Efthymios Symeou

Medieval Collection
Earthenware hand-painted and
glazed plate
D 10 ½ inches
Dishwasher safe
Source: Cyprus Handicraft Center

White Collection
Earthenware vase
Custom-made to any size
Dishwasher safe
Artist: Myro Psara

White Collection
Earthenware vase
Custom-made to any size
Dishwasher safe
Artist: Myro Psara

White Dove Collection
Earthenware vase
Custom-made to any size
Artist: Myro Psara

Medieval Collection
Earthenware hand-painted and glazed
Set of four
Dishwasher safe
Source: Cyprus Handicraft Center

Wedding Collection
Earthenware
Dishwasher safe
Artist: Myro Psara

Dove Collection
Earthenware hand-painted
Dishwasher safe
Artist: Myro Psara

OVERLEAF These one-of-a-kind, hand-painted, and signed colorful plates are the work of Sakis Dorites, a Cypriot artist who has been creating ceramic art since the age of 14.

# CATALOG

Textiles are all handmade either by needle, lace, crochet, or embroidery. Cottons are woven on a traditional Cypriot loom. They can be found at Cyprus Handicraft Center, and are often custom-made. All items have been chosen by Helen in Cyprus.

Aegean Collection
Stoneware hand-painted cups
H 4 inches
Available individually or as a set of 2 or 3
Dishwasher safe
Source: Cyprus Handicraft Center

Psari Collection
Earthenware hand-painted
Dishwasher Safe
Artist: Myro Psara

Pontus Plate
W 9 inches
Stoneware
Dishwasher safe
Artist: Efthymios Symeou

Collection of various tablecloths
and blankets
All hand-woven cotton on a Cypriot loom

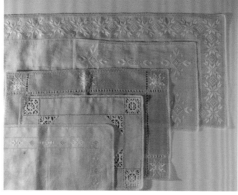

Lefkaritiko placemats and runner
Various designs of Lefkaritiko lace
hand made on linen
Placemats: 17 x 12 inches;
Runner: 16 x 35 inches

Lefkonoitziatiko tablecloth in large size
Cotton woven on a Cypriot loom
90 x 84½ inches
Available in placemats, runners, and
other sizes

Striped cotton tablecloths
Traditional Cypriot tablecloth woven
on loom
54 x 78 inches

Lefkonoitziatiko typical multicoloured
bedspread or tablecloth
Cotton woven on a Cypriot loom
63 x 94½ inches; available in other sizes
Origin: Lefkonoiko Village
(in occupied Cyprus)

Woven blanket
Cotton woven on a Cypriot loom
73 x 52 inches

# CATALOG

Because of the complexity of the designs, sufficient time is needed to produce each piece depending on size. All items can be sold per piece or as sets of two unless otherwise stated. Sizes and colors may vary slightly.

Organic Collection
Stoneware inlay design
Small, medium, large
Dishwasher safe
Artist: Oria Petropoulou

Traditional wine/water jugs
Glazed earthenware made in Cyprus
H 6 inches
Available individually or in multiples
Dishwasher safe

Aegean collection
Stoneware hand-painted dinner plate
10 inches
Dishwasher safe
Source: Cyprus Handicraft Center

Phythkiotika placemats in various designs
Woven and embroidered
12 x 18 inches
Origin: Fyti Village, Paphos

Veniz lace tablecloth
Handmade
Available in various sizes

Lavender-filled dolls with
embroidery detail

Kourelloudes placemats
Typical Cypriot woven technique;
various fabrics

Lefkaritiko placemat
Handmade lace on linen
Origin: Lefkara Village

Veniz lace, round mat, handmade

# INDEX

# INDEX

FRONT COVER Antoine Bootz photographed all the elements of a happy life: family, art, and good food. The ceramics and textiles are handmade by Cypriot artists and artisans.

BACK COVER The outside dining area of Helen's house in Serifos is a preferred spot for lazy afternoons and lively evenings.

ENDPAPERS This fragment of handmade lace is from Cyprus.

HALF TITLE PAGE AND OPPOSITE TITLE PAGE In Serifos, Helen always keeps a sweet-smelling basil plant on the windowsill in her kitchen.

OPPOSITE CONTENTS Helen often likes to fill a ceramic head by Greek artist Anna Antonopoulou with fresh flowers.

*Helen Tsanos Sheinman* was raised in London, England, by Cypriot parents. She graduated from King's College, London, with a B.A. in philosophy, modern Greek literature, and linguistic studies. Currently, she is committed to volunteering in areas relating to human rights and education. Helen learned to cook at a young age and loves to spend time preparing meals for her family and friends. This is her first book.

# ACKNOWLEDGMENTS

To families everywhere who have known the joys and difficulties of growing up in a new country, yet have managed to hold on to their unique heritages and traditions around food in the face of a changing environment; to the families that sit around the table, meal after meal, celebrating the fact that there is no greater pleasure than living a life filled with love, laughter, and enjoying good food together. May we all continue to eat with those we love.

Food, like life, can take you in any and every direction. It has the power to transport you to far off lands, to remind you of the happiest times and the saddest moments, to take you on distant adventures, and to welcome you home. As with life, food is not good if it is untouched—it needs the joy and spirit of company in order to flourish. It is those whom I love, and those for whom I have had the good fortune of cooking, that are truly the special ingredient in all of my recipes. If any one of these people had been absent from my life, this book and all that it stands for would never have been imagined.

To my husband, Andrew, *above right*, I owe it all to you. For the joy and laughter, the creativity and style, the courage and freedom, and, above all, the love, passion, and security that make everything in my life worthwhile.

To my daughters, Alexia and Isabel, for being both my right and left hands. Isabel, your writing and editing skills were invaluable to me. Alexia, from the start you shared your clever and creative insights and really helped me see it all through to the end. You are both my pillars of strength and the source of my joy and playfulness.

To Glen Senk and Keith Johnson, for being the best of friends and sharing with me your boundless generosity, unassuming intellect, and youthful energy for over 30 years. Thank you so much for giving me the opportunity and encouragement to step out into the world to see what I could find. It was while filming *Man Shops Globe* in Cyprus with Keith that I was first inspired to create this book, and I've never looked back. You both have always believed in me, and this project came about because of the two of you.

To my cousin Christina Tsanos and her husband, Mihalis Panayidou, who were pivotal companions in my exploration of Cypriot food and art. Thank you for your endless patience, kindness, and loving support throughout our travels together.

To the Cypriot artists Yiannos Anastasiou, Julia Astreou Christoforou, Sakis Dorites, Oria Petropoulou, Myro Psara, Efthymios Symeou, and the Cyprus Handicraft Centers, for their unique and visionary creations.

To every single member of my family in London, Cyprus, and Greece, I need not name you individually because every page of this book was written with, for, and because of you. You are, always have been, and always will be my inspiration. Each of you has contributed to my story in your own unique and fundamental ways. I am looking forward to continuing with all of you by my side.

To my amazingly dear, loyal, and fun friends, without whose presence I would not have known how truly wonderful life, friendship, and food could be. A big thank you in particular to Martha Baker, Jeff Baron, Susan Boland, Maritza Chateau, Connie Emmerich, Kelly Granat, John Hartz, Sophie Kasselakis, Yong Kwok, Brendon Lynch, Michael Morrison, Nadine Morrison, Bobbi Queen, Eve Silver, Anne Stark, and Marjorie Suna, who all allowed me to ramble, rant, and write, and always kept me laughing. A special thank you to Mara Manus for being the very first one to insist that I photograph my recipes and table settings.

To everyone behind the making of this book: It would never have been possible and so meaningfully and beautifully put together had it not been for your collaborative talents and expertise.

Special thanks to: Stafford Cliff, for his ingenious artistic direction, and Dominick J. Santise, Jr., for his dedication in producing this book. To Joseph Chevront, for testing every recipe meticulously and for flattering me by adopting some of them into his permanent repertoire.

To the Pointed Leaf Press team: Suzanne Slesin, my publisher, editor, and dear friend, who made me laugh and cry while showing me the art of discipline and the benefits of true organization, but, most importantly, the joy of putting thoughts down on paper and helping me write what was really in my heart; and Regan Toews, Deanna Kawitzky, Marion D.S. Dreyfus, and Nyasha Gutsa, for their patience in seeing every detail through from beginning to end.

To the gifted photographers and stylists with whom I had the pleasure of working: Antoine Bootz and Rebecca Omweg, for their help in so beautifully illustrating the ideas and recipes; Costas Picadas, who captured the true essence of Serifos, Greece; Christopher Lawrence and Garry Wade, who, through their talent and precision, produced the images for the catalog; and Viki Ortiz, who helped me create the spectacular rose-covered wedding cake. To Maritza Chateau and Alexia Sheinman—thank you for allowing me to include some of your beautiful photographs in this book.

To all of my daughters' friends, who never cease to inspire me with their interests and passions, and are always the willing guinea pigs of my recipes. Thank you in particular to Jenny Bright, Brooke Elmlinger, Natalie Suna, and Elizabeth Tabak, for their kind words; to Emilios Pavli, who, with his musical lyrics, continues to remind me of my brother Lysandros; and last but not least, Claire Suna, who will in no time, I predict, have her own recipe books. You have all contributed in so many ways to *Love, Laughter, and Lunch*. Helen Tsanos Sheinman, New York, September 2011

Pointed Leaf Press, LLC.
136 Baxter Street
New York, NY 10013
www.pointedleafpress.com

Pointed Leaf Press is pleased to offer special discounts for our publications and can provide signed copies upon request. Please contact info@pointedleafpress.com for details.

Printed and bound in Thailand
First edition
10 9 8 7 6 5 4 3 2 1
Library of Congress Control Number: 2011925226
ISBN 13: 978-0-9833889-2-0